KT-479-796

Also by The F2

F2: *World of Football*

F2: *Football Academy*

F2: *Galaxy of Football*

F2 WORLD CLASS

Published by Blink Publishing
2.25, The Plaza,
535 Kings Road,
Chelsea Harbour,
London, SW10 0SZ

www.blinkpublishing.co.uk

facebook.com/blinkpublishing
twitter.com/blinkpublishing

Flexibind - 9781788700269
Ebook - 9781788700276
Paperback - 9781788701020

A CIP catalogue of this book is available from the British Library.

Design by Steve Leard
Printed and bound in Italy

1 3 5 7 9 10 8 6 4 2

Blink Publishing is an imprint of the Bonnier Publishing Group
www.bonnierpublishing.co.uk

For The F2 Family,
you're in a class of your own.

THE F2 APP

GET THE ULTIMATE FOOTBALL SKILLS GUIDE FREE ON YOUR SCREEN!

Billy: Download our free F2 App and you'll be able to see our skills come to life on your device.

Jez: That's right, we've packed in new, never-before-seen video tutorials and helpful tips so you can learn how to play like a pro. And once you've honed your touch you can upload your own skill videos and share them with us!

Billy: To access all this exclusive content download the free app from the iTunes App Store or Google Play Store, launch the app and point your device's camera at the pages with the special phone icon (right). Then sit back and watch the magic happen!

Jez: It's that simple, so what are you waiting for? Download, read, watch, learn and take your game to the next level. See you on the football pitch!

*The F2 App by The F2 requires an Internet connection to be downloaded and can be used on iPhone, iPad or Android devices. For direct links to download the app and further information, visit www.blinkpublishing.co.uk

Scan this page now for your first video!

CONTENTS

INTRO

WELCOME TO F2: WORLD CLASS

Yes guys!

Do you want to elevate your skills? Are you ready to take your game to a whole new level? Do you want to become the best you can?

Then you've come to the right place. Before you turn through the pages ahead, set your intention to maximise every single asset you have in the quest to reach elite level. Then work your way through this book, which is your all-access pass to the secrets of the stars.

We will walk you through the different routes to the top. First, we will define 'world class'. What does it even mean? What separates your Kanes from your Can'ts your Messi from just messy?

We'll take you through the important zones you need to work on: mentality, strength, skill and recovery. Want to know how to improve all of these? Keep reading, people.

Then we'll look at your diet, tactical awareness and motivation. We'll blend simple but effective tips with our own memories and stories, sprinkling in some gold dust from some of the game's biggest names.

You know, not all the action takes place on the pitch any more – so we will show you how to create a brand. From our experiences creating the F2 and Rascal brands we have learned so much. We want to share it with you, the F2 Family.

And check this out: all that is only the beginning of this brilliant book. We'll discuss some of our favourite players in the Tekkers Masters sections. From Kylian Mbappé to Marcus Rashford, from Harry Kane to David de Gea, we have a good old chat about what makes these legends tick.

This freestyle fantasy-land also includes our guide to nailing various skills, including the Triple Elastico, the Suárez Heel Flick and the Ronaldo Chop.

Want to relax after all that graft? Then enter the F2 World of Fun, including quizzes, word searches and other puzzles. Then, in Billy v Jezza, we debate the hot topics of international football and give you the chance to get involved.

So what are you waiting for? Turn the page and get ready to get better.

Love, peace and tekkers,
Billy and Jez, aka The F2

F2
CHAPTER
ONE

F2: WORLD CLASS

SETTING THE BAR

Billy: Okay Jez, let's get right down to business. In this book we're going to show the F2 Family how to be world class. So what exactly does it mean to be 'world class'? Where are we setting the bar on this one? Sum it up nice and easily for us...

Jez: Hahaha! Cheers, Bill, ping me a nice easy question early doors, why don't you?

Billy: Well, you know me: I love to bring others into the game...

Jez: Very generous of you. Look, I'd say there are several qualities. A player is world class when they are operating at the peak of the game . You have to consider the level they play at, their skills, their athleticism, their degree of consistency and a range of other factors including their mental strength and how they fare in the biggest games.

There's a lot there. You don't just become world class because you're good in one or two areas.

Billy: So let's start breaking these down. For sure, consistency is important. If you can put in an eight-out-of-ten performance every few games or so, then you're doing good. You can afford to be pleased with yourself.

But the world-class players put in shifts as good as that or better in every single game. These are the worldies, these are the winners. That killer consistency takes you a long way to joining the top most tier of the game.

Jez: Yeah, and doing that sort of business in the biggest games is also part of it. We hear a lot of talk about 'big game players' and that's because it's important – and the higher you go in the game the more important it becomes.

If you play well and take your team to a big final or league decider, that's all well and good. But if you bottle it on the big day you're not going to get yourself into the world-class bracket. And trust me – sometimes big-name players just can't hack it when the pressure noose is at its tightest!

Billy: Are you going to name some names?

Jez: No chance! To do the biz when the pressure is at its most intense you have to be brave, too. So courage is another world-class attribute. And listen, this doesn't just mean physical courage when the tackles are flying in. It also means mental courage. You need to be someone who sees the game when the stakes are unbelievably high and says: I'll have some of that!

Billy: So, are we saying you have to have won big honours to be world class? I'm not sure we are. Look at Harry Kane. He's clearly one of the best strikers in the world at the moment by any measure. Yes, he's missing a trophy in his cabinet, but that doesn't lessen his ability. And I'm sure those trophies and accolades will arrive sooner rather than later.

Jez: Sergio Ramos and Neymar are very different kinds of players. David de Gea is different again to both of them. But all three of them are arguably world class because of their talent and application to the game. No world-class player is ever satisfied – they keep striving every day to improve.

And there are very few world-class players around. It's a term that gets applied to players way too easily. I reckon there's only about a dozen at the moment.

So what we're saying is this: to be world class you'd have to be in the first eleven not just of your club, not even of your national side – but also your planet.

Billy: Spot on! If Earth was drawn against Mars in the Universe Cup, the team that represented this planet would be comprised of the world-class players we have. If you're not making the cut in that team, you're not world class.

So that's what being world class means for the top professionals in the game. But does it mean something different for the rest of us, Jez?

Jez: Mate, what are you today – the quizmaster? Why don't you answer the question this time?

Billy: Fair comment. Well, I think that for the rest of us what we're doing is striving to become world class. Becoming world class is all about a certain attitude, or a state of mind. Your first mental challenge is to want to be the best. That starts with being the best on your team, then in your league, then in your county and so on. How can you ever become the best unless you aim for the very top?

Jez: So true.

Billy: It's about thinking big and being realistic, all at the same time. Like, we can't all have Lionel Messi's talent...

Jez: Oh, come on. I think you sell yourself short there, mate...

Billy: All right, pipe down. What I'm saying is we can't all have Lionel Messi's talent but we can all have his dedication, focus, positivity and work ethic.

So let's draw a line right here and say that for us and for this book we're focusing on becoming world class, which begins with being the very best you can be.

Jez: And that can start with watching world-class players very carefully. If you want to play football for a living and reach their level, thanks to television and the internet you've got this amazing opportunity to sit in the comfort of your own home and study the very best in the world at what you want to do.

With most industries in the world it won't be possible for you to do that. You'd need some sort of special 'in', or elite inside knowledge. They are not open and available to the masses.

With football it's all there to be seen week in, week out. You can watch Lionel Messi play every week and learn from him. Use this access, don't let it slip through your fingers. Study the pros, learn from them, try and be like them.

Billy: Yes, I'd say to any kid trying to make it, watch as much top-level football as you can. Just do it. Everything you watch you will take in, even if it's subliminally. And then when you go out on the pitch it can influence you in a positive way.

In the pages ahead we are going to show you how to elevate your skills. We will take you through the different qualities you need to work on if you want to become the best you can be.

So let's get down to it.

TEKKERS MASTERS: KYLIAN MBAPPÉ

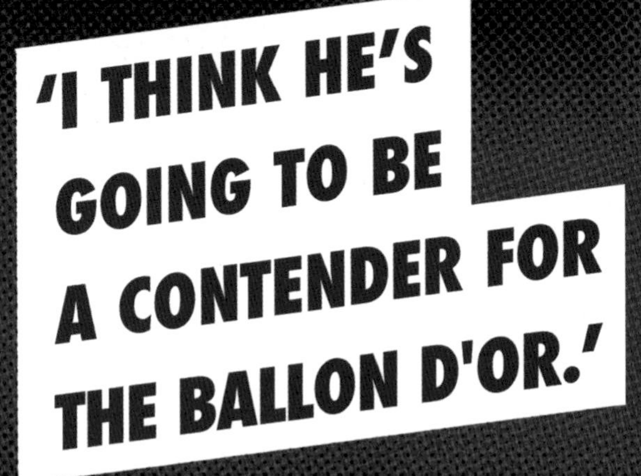

'I THINK HE'S GOING TO BE A CONTENDER FOR THE BALLON D'OR.'

Jez: You know what? Since Neymar first burst onto the scene at Barcelona I don't think there has been a new, young player coming through as exciting as Mbappé. And I actually think these two guys have got a lot in common.

He's training alongside Neymar pretty much every day so he's in the best position you could be. It's a dream situation for him because outside of Lionel Messi and Cristiano Ronaldo, Neymar is probably the next player you'd want to be learning from.

Billy: I agree with that.

Jez: They play in similar positions, don't they? So I think Mbappé can really push on and learn a lot from Neymar. It's so exciting. I can't wait to see how good he can become because I think he's going to be a contender for the Ballon d'Or once Messi and Ronaldo retire. I really think that.

Billy: Strong words but I know what you mean. He's got the complete package. When you look at his all-round game, he's your ideal striker because he's got a bit of everything.

His judgement is strong. All the top strikers in the world know what the right options in each moment are. They've got the skills and they know just when to make the right move.

Jez: I remember a great move from him against Caen. When he got the ball he was in space but then two Caen players tried to close him down. He just blasted past both of them. See ya later!

He sped down the right and then polished off the move by sending a pinpoint pass to Cavani, who backheeled it into the net. And get this – this was on Mbappé's 19th birthday. He's still so young, man.

Billy: Another of his assets is a low centre of gravity.

Jez: What does that mean, Bill? Maybe you'd better break it down for everyone.

Billy: Sure. Most skilful players have a low centre of gravity. It means they have good balance and the ability to ride tackles.

So look at players like Diego Maradona or Sergio Aguero. These guys can ride tackles and still stay on their feet. Their balance is exceptional.

To have that attribute is such a positive, because when you're dribbling you can be more agile. When someone is tackling you, you can get out of situations by twisting and turning. All the top dribblers have incredibly low centres of gravity.

Jez: That's right. Most times, that comes through being small. If you look at Aguero, Coutinho and others they're not huge. Mbappé is not small, and yet he still has it. So that's a great combination.

He actually reminds me of Thierry Henry a little bit. They're both big guys and extremely fast. I remember it being said about Henry that he could potentially be a professional sprinter. As far as I know, the same applies to Mbappé. He scored a goal against Lille where he ran from the halfway line and his speed was clocked at 36kph, which is getting close to Usain Bolt speed.

Also he's fast with and without the ball, which is more rare than you'd think. Some players are faster without the ball. They struggle to carry the ball at their top speed but Mbappé has no problem with that.

'HE ACTUALLY REMINDS ME OF THIERRY HENRY A LITTLE BIT.'

Billy: He seems mentally mature, too.

Jez: Yeah, he must be, he must be. Neymar's the same. For them to have achieved what they have achieved at such a young age, well, you look at other 17 and 18-year-olds and a lot of them are just finishing school, not really applying themselves to anything, low on confidence.

And look, that's kind of normal for a teenage boy. They are often a bit insecure and short of self-confidence. But this guy, you don't see that. It's like he's got a different mindset. I don't know if it's them or their parents or the football club...or is it just an inherent, supreme self-confidence?

I'm really not sure, but I wasn't blessed with any of that myself. When I was his age, I wasn't self-confident, I'll tell you that for nothing.

Billy: You, short of confidence? That's a tad hard to imagine now.

Jez: I don't know what you mean!

GET THE SKILLS: PIRLO PING

FACT FILE

ORIGIN: UNKNOWN
SKILL TYPE: PASS
DIFFICULTY RATING: 5
TEKKERS RATING: 7
FREQUENTLY USED BY: PIRLO, KROOS, POGBA, BECKHAM

Billy: The Ping pass is one of my favourite ways to pass the ball. If you're a midfield playmaker you can use this to get great distance without needing too much power, perfect for when you need to switch direction of play from one side of the pitch to the other. No one was better at this than Andrea Pirlo, the Italian pass master. I remember when we met him, he demonstrated it for us – it was unreal how accurate he was!

It's a direct drive with no swaz or curl on it at all, maybe just a touch of backspin so that it flies straight like an arrow. It should be nice and easy for the receiver to control it. The key is to make the right connection – you can hear the ping – with the ball. You don't need to hit it hard. If you hit it right, trust me, the ball will travel. Pure Ping perfection. Like Pirlo.

F2
RUN-UP AT A 45-DEGREE ANGLE
PLANT YOUR NON-STRIKING
BOOT NEXT TO THE BALL
STRIKE JUST BELOW MID-BALL
WITH THE BONE OF YOUR FOOT
FOLLOW THROUGH
THE BALL SHOULD FLY STRAIGHT TO
YOUR TEAM-MATE WITH NO SPIN
EVEN WITHOUT MUCH POWER
THE BALL SHOULD FLY FAR

BILLY V JEZZA

FAVOURITE KIT

Yes guys! Us two work together all year round but for this section we want to go head-to-head. We are going to thrash out which goals, kits and other matches we like best from World Cups down the years. Each topic gives you a chance to join in the debate. So tweet us @TheF2 and lets us know which of us you agree with! #TeamJezza or #TeamBilly.

Billy: The thing is, I really like white kits like Germany and Real Madrid have had for so long. There's just something special about them - they are so iconic and identifiable. Over the decades they have become synonymous with swagger and class. It wouldn't be the same with a Sunday league team somehow.

Jez: Yeah, there's something so pure about a white football kit. I'd agree with that actually. It almost feels spiritual. That Real kit that's all white with gold trimming is just a touch of class.

Billy: That's right, it's an absolute peach. Holland and Argentina are two other sides that always have classic kits. Again, it's all about the identity, isn't it? You know Holland will be in that iconic orange and Argentina in the sky blue and white stripes.

But let's get down to business: my favourite clobber of all time, I think, was the fresh white shirts of Germany at the 2010 World Cup. The ones with the black piping. That kit wins it for me.

Jez: That's a real good one Bill but I'm going with the classic Adidas France kit of 1998! I was 10 and I remember that tournament so well being an Arsenal fan. I can see it all now: Patrick Vieira and Emmanuel Petit combining to score the opening goal of the World Cup Final. It was an amazing kit.

It's all so vivid from that summer. I also remember Zidane wearing the Predator Accelerators and wheeling away in celebration. I loved the red of the kit matching detail on his boots. Yeah, France's 1998 World Cup-winning kit is my winning kit.

#TeamBilly: Germany 2010

#TeamJezza: France 1998

You: ____________________

TANGO

F2
CHAPTER
TWO
TANGO

F2: WORLD CLASS

THE KIT

Jez: So we know what being world class means, but what do we need to get there?

Billy: You're right, Jez – I suppose you could say that the private jet is taxiing down the runway, we're travelling world class, but have we packed our bags?

Jez: Ha! Have we switched off our electronic devices?

Billy: Are we ready for take-off?

Jez: Oh yes, Bill, but before we hit the heights, let's run through the checklist one last time. Here's the kit you'll need if you're planning to be world class:

Boots – mould and stud

Billy: Sometimes, although a game is scheduled to take place on grass, at the last minute it's changed to 3G. So we reckon you should bring both pairs of boots to games.

Spare studs

Jez: This is important as no one wants to be a stud or two down when trying to balance.

Shin pads

Billy: For any opposed practice, wear shin pads to provide protection. Even training can be high tempo so knocks and contact are inevitable.

Pad stays

Jez: Most pads come now with a tube that goes over the leg and the pad to ensure the pad doesn't move. We like to be as comfortable as possible when playing the game and this stops pads slipping and sliding around our socks.

Base layer

Billy: A lot of players wear a short-sleeved shirt so a base layer is key in summer to keep cool and in winter to keep warm. It provides support and it can be more comfortable to wear a base layer with short-sleeved shirt than a long-sleeved shirt.

Sock tape

Jez: This must be the same colour as game-day socks.

Vicks VapoRub

Billy: A bit of an 'old-school' one but a lot of the players add a rub of Vicks to their shirts when playing games especially in the cold. It helps them breathe more easily.

Under socks

Jez: These are especially important if you wear a sock or a grip sock under the club colour sock. We normally wear short socks over the top of our football socks. This provides support and often packs the boot more for comfort and protection.

Toiletries

Billy: You need a shower after a game. So make sure you have your wash bag containing shower gel, sponge, deodorant and talcum powder for aching feet!

Flip flops/sliders

Jez: These are essential to wear around the changing room and in and out of the showers/physio room.

Plasters

Billy: You can keep these in your bag in case of blisters and/or to cover any jewellery.

Towel

Jez: Every player needs one of these.

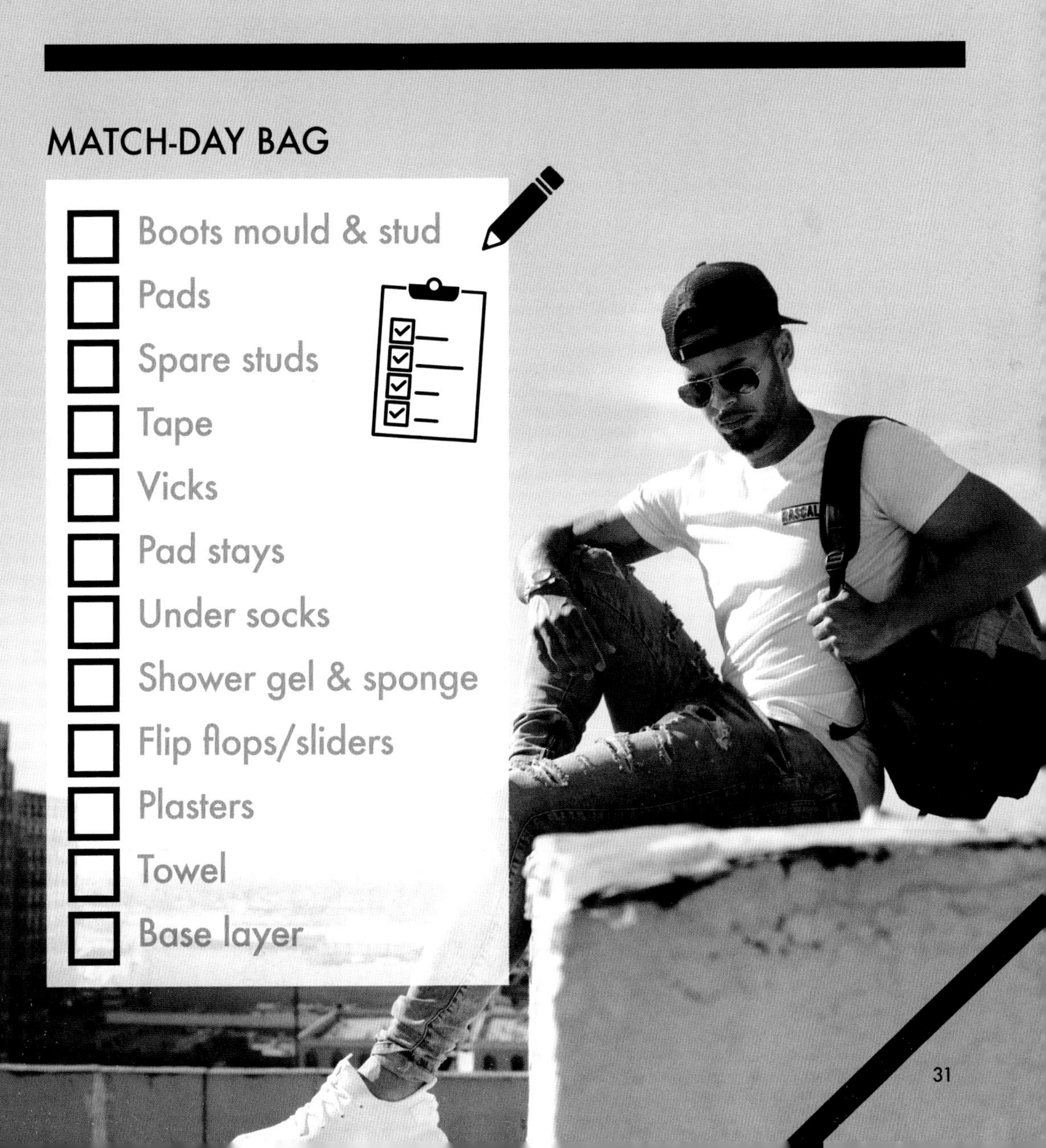

MATCH-DAY BAG

- [ ] Boots mould & stud
- [ ] Pads
- [ ] Spare studs
- [ ] Tape
- [ ] Vicks
- [ ] Pad stays
- [ ] Under socks
- [ ] Shower gel & sponge
- [ ] Flip flops/sliders
- [ ] Plasters
- [ ] Towel
- [ ] Base layer

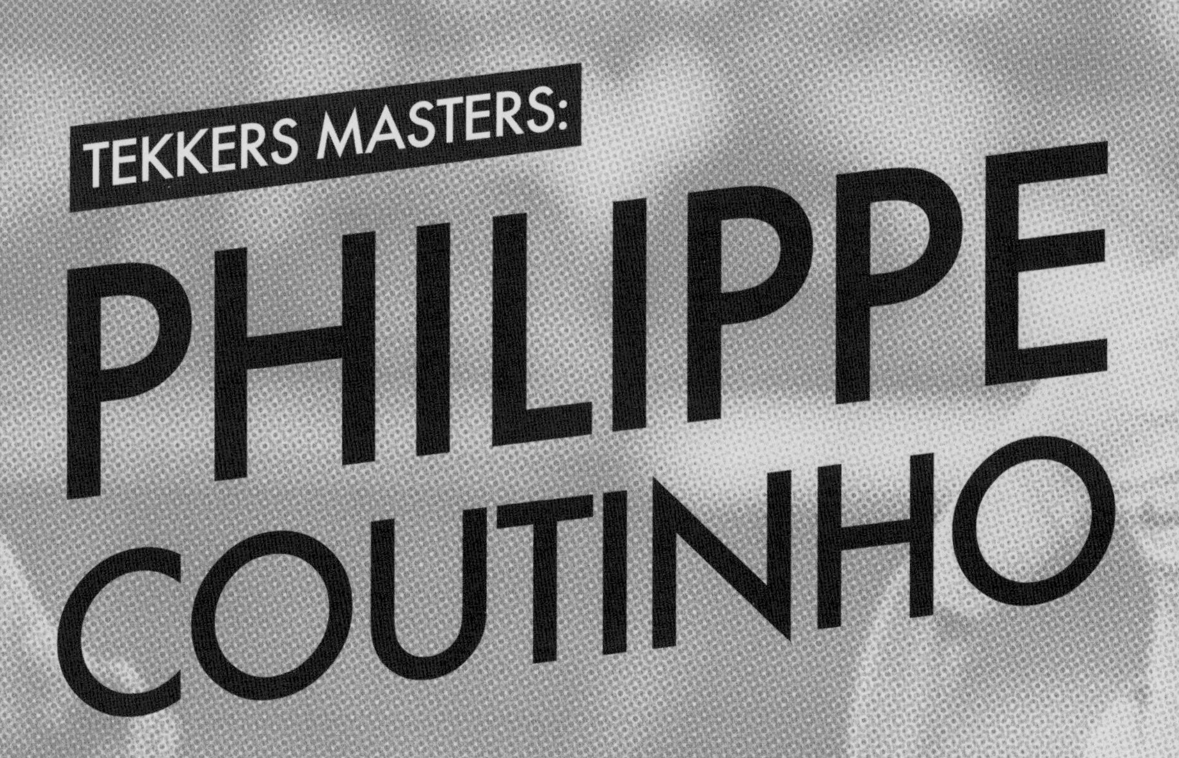

TEKKERS MASTERS: PHILIPPE COUTINHO

'THIS GUY IS WHAT YOU WOULD CALL A MATCH WINNER.'

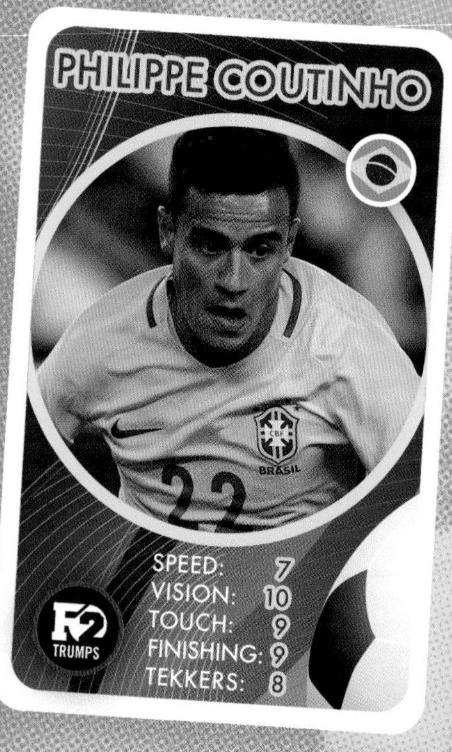

Billy: This guy is what you would call a match winner - as simple as. There are certain players in the world that you can rely on to do that, to be a match winner. You could be up against them in the World Cup final and everything is going your team's way, but then suddenly they turn the game on its head.

Every team needs that one person to step up on the big stage, and who has such ability that when everything is going wrong against you, he can do that one piece of magic to win you that game, to win you that World Cup, or whichever trophy it is.

It's a very hard thing to have because there's not many people who can change the game on their own. They may contribute or score a goal but this is something different we are talking about. We are talking about a player who can turn a game on its head.

That's what Coutinho is all about for me. He's a match winner.

Jez: I really like him and I expect him to absolutely smash it for Barcelona in La Liga. He was already top, top notch at Liverpool, so now he's surrounded by top-class players, I honestly think he's going to go to a new level. I think he was made for the Spanish league.

Liverpool fans won't be glad he left but I think for Coutinho himself, and for neutrals, it is an exciting move.

Billy: Yeah, I think he could go on to be better than Neymar. I really do. It's a bold statement, I realise. But I think he'll be a revelation. He was exceptional at Liverpool but with the right players around him, he will flourish, he really will.

How do you like him to line up, Jez?

Jez: Well, he's versatile, isn't he? But I think I like him as a good, Brazilian-style number 10. In the last four years in the Prem, no one has scored more goals than Coutinho from outside the box, so he's great from distance. He's actually a prime example of a number 10.

From that part of the park, he can wreak havoc. He's so tricky, you can't get the ball off him, and he's got good vision. He'll give you assists as well as the goals. What more can you ask for from a forward?

Billy: Indeed! They call him the magician and I'm not surprised, because that's what he is. He can create magic on the football pitch. He's one of those special talents that makes you sit up and take notice. He gets on the ball and the excitement builds. You just know he's going to create something.

This is because in his armoury of talent, he can do so much. He can hit a 40 or 50-yard ball. He's got all the skills we've talked about on our videos and in our books. He can

'HE'S SO TRICKY, YOU CAN'T GET THE BALL OFF HIM, AND HE'S GOT GOOD VISION.'

swaz it, he can whip it, he can knuckle. He can twist, he can turn, he can accelerate.

Also, he can score outrageous long-distance shots. The technique he has for that is similar to Ronaldinho. He's been compared with him a lot and at first, I must say I didn't see it. Ronaldinho is a player who means so much to me. I'm hesitant to compare anyone to him.

But when I think about it, there are some comparisons to be had. You know that anywhere in that last third, even if they're 30 yards out, it's scoring territory for these two guys.

So how do you defend against people like Coutinho and Ronaldinho? If you go tight, he'll destroy you one-on-one. He's incredibly intelligent with his movement. But if you stand off he

can get his shot off. It's so difficult to know what the right thing is to do. He was a big, big loss for Liverpool.

Jez: Look, the harsh truth is that he was always going to leave Anfield for La Liga. It's the same with players like Harry Kane and Dele Alli at Spurs. Chances are they'll be in Spain before too long.

Billy: Watch it, Gooner!

Jez: Hahaha!

GET THE SKILLS:

RONALDINHO BACK TOUCH

FACT FILE

ORIGIN: UNKNOWN
SKILL TYPE: CONTROL
DIFFICULTY RATING: 7
TEKKERS RATING: 9
FREQUENTLY USED BY: RONALDINHO, NEYMAR

Jez: Here's some tekkers to get the crowd on its feet. I saw Neymar do this shortly after he arrived at PSG, and it was good, I mean, he followed it up with a rainbow flick, so it was pretty special. But, for me the master will always be Ronaldinho. The original and the best.

The trick here is to set up as if to chest control the ball, and then spin at the last and take the ball on your back. As the ball hits you need to drop down quickly to take the speed off the ball and kill it. And, trust me, you've definitely killed it!

F2
SET UP TO RECEIVE THE BALL ON
YOUR CHEST
AT THE LAST MOMENT SPIN
CUSHION THE BALL ON
YOUR BACK
NAILED IT

SET UP FOR THE CHEST CONTROL

START TO SPIN

KEEP YOUR EYES ON THE BALL TO THE LAST SECOND
CROUCH TO CUSHION THE BALL
ALLOW IT BOUNCE OVER YOUR HEAD
LET THE CROWD GO WILD!

BILLY V JEZZA

WORLD XI

Jez: This is so tough...how far do you go back for this one? Pele, Maradona, Eusebio, Cruyff! So many names. Wow, okay let's have a go at this:

#TeamJezza:

GK: Manuel Neuer
RB: Cafu
CB: Paolo Maldini
CB: Carles Puyol
LB: Roberto Carlos
CDM: Vieira
CM: Scholes
CAM: Zidane
RF: Henry
CF: Ronaldo R9
LF: Lionel Messi

NEUER
CAFU
PUYOL
MALDINI
ROBERTO CARLOS
ZIDANE
VIEIRA
SCHOLES
HENRY
MESSI
RONALDO R9

Billy: What a team that is Jez! That's tough to beat.... but how about:

#TeamBilly:

GK: Buffon
CB: Philip Lahm
CB: Sergio Ramos
CB: Paolo Maldini
CDM: Pirlo
CM: Xavi
RM: Ronaldinho
CAM: Zidane
LM: Lionel Messi
CF: Maradona
CF: Ronaldo CR7

Jez: Imagine putting those two teams against each other. What a game that would be!!!

#TeamYou:

1 Kahn
2 Maldini
3 Badbuster ¿ German
4 Marcelo
5 Carlos
6 Zidane
7 Modric
8 Ronaldo CR7
9 Pele
10 Maradona
11 Ronaldo R9

cheeky little
RASCAL

CHAPTER
THREE

F2: WORLD CLASS

MENTAL AGILITY

Billy: I think this is such an important chapter. Because, you know, you have to be really careful what you let into your head. Particularly these days, when there's so much information coming at you on social media – news, opinions, punditry.

Jez: Agreed. So here's a really good tip for you guys to improve your game. Years ago, a coach told me: 'Jez, sometimes, when you're watching a game of football, turn the volume down. Put it on mute.'

It worked: when you deprive one sense, it enhances the others. With the volume off, your eyes and your mind can absorb things that you might have missed otherwise.

Of course sometimes the commentary team can give you an insight, or pick up on a detail that may have passed you by, but I'd say it's worth giving this a try.

So yeah, I occasionally hit that mute button and I'm telling you, it really works. You see the game differently. You're not influenced by anyone else's opinion. You're just watching it in silence. I found it really effective.

Billy: Put your phone down during the match, too. Don't look at social media during games. Don't make the TV your second screen – make it your only screen. Focus on the game. Make it everything. You'll only get out of it what you put in.

Jez: So let's turn to visualisation. I've seen studies that say that if you blend mental imagery with repetitive training you can actually create patterns within your brain. Physically!

Wayne Rooney is proof of the power of visualisation. He said that part of his preparation for a game is to ask the kit man which colour kit the team will be wearing, so he knows what to picture in his head.

He said that the night before the game, he visualises himself scoring and playing really well. He said he's done this his whole life. How he put it was: 'You're trying to put yourself in that moment and trying to prepare yourself.'

Billy: That's right. But as Wayne said himself, it's important that you visualise realistic things. It would be easy to imagine yourself scoring your 10th goal from the halfway line in a 10–0 win in the World Cup. That's probably a tad far.

I know that Jose Mourinho believes in re-creating the exact conditions of match day during training. He takes specific scenarios and then acts them out methodically on the training field.

He said: 'I predict the maximum I can, the different aspects of the game and the different directions that the game can follow, and I try to prepare them better than ever.'

Better than ever? He isn't even joking: he said there are at least a thousand different scenarios he trains his teams for. So anything from a wide man being parked in the corner by three defenders, to his team being suddenly hit by a wave of pressing. Whatever goes on out there, he's taken them through it on the training field.

Jez: Man, that's visualisation taken to the extreme! So, readers, you can do your own version down the park with your mates. Work through as many of the likely match-day situations as you can. Make a list of common scenarios when you watch a game and then practise them down the park. You'll be prepared for pretty much anything that comes your way.

Billy: It's all about picturing it in your head. There are different types of players out there. There are those who dream of making it into the first team, those who dream about winning matches, and those who dream about winning trophies. Then, if you want to talk world class, there are those who dream about being the star man as their team wins the top trophies.

Jez: Set your visualisation at the (realistic) level you want it – because that level you're imagining in your mind might just be the level you reach in real life!

Billy: As Mourinho does, keep practising and imagining specific scenarios – and watch your confidence soar. I can't think of a better example of this than David Beckham. He said that when he went to take the corners which led to the equaliser and winning goal in the 1999 Champions League final, he didn't feel any pressure.

Even though it was the last moments of the Champions League final, with his side trailing 1–0, he had practised these corners so many times that he could go into those crucial two moments full of confidence. And guess what? His team score twice from those corners and he lifts the Champions League trophy.

Jez: And just like you can prepare for a game with visualisation in your head, you can also wind down from a game or training session by literally watching what happened. A really good way of developing your technique is by getting video footage of yourself and studying it meticulously.

And I mean meticulously – you have to really hyper-analyse yourself. This means being super honest with yourself over what you think you've done wrong.

So here's how to go about it. Ask a friend, coach or family member to film you. It's easy, they can do it on a phone. Then sit down with a top coach, or anyone you trust who knows their stuff, and do a truly fearless 'player analysis' on yourself. Look at what you did right, what you did wrong. Be like the top pundits on Sky Sports – but judging yourself!

Billy: That's right, Jez. Discuss what you see with the coach. You need to find someone who knows what they're talking about and is prepared to be honest with you. In the same way, you yourself need to be ready to hear honest feedback. So you need to be able to trust one another.

Jez: As well as studying yourself, you can study the best players in the world. For instance, some players are known for having incredible movement. Dele Alli would be one, Sergio Aguero is another. So watch them on and off the ball. There's so much footage on the internet you can use.

Billy: Basically, whichever position you play, study the best players in the world in that position. Just do what they do – you can't go wrong!

Jez: You can't go wrong as long as you put in the hours. I mean, football is a random game where no two games are alike – a bit like snowflakes. But there are still general patterns that keep repeating. Practise for those patterns, like Mourinho's teams do.

If you do enough studying of the best players in the world, when those patterns arise in your game, you can try and do the same as they did. It might sound like basic advice but it's good advice.

Billy: Good shout. Be methodical. As well as putting in the time on the field, put the time in at home as well.

Jez: And remember – keep visualising!

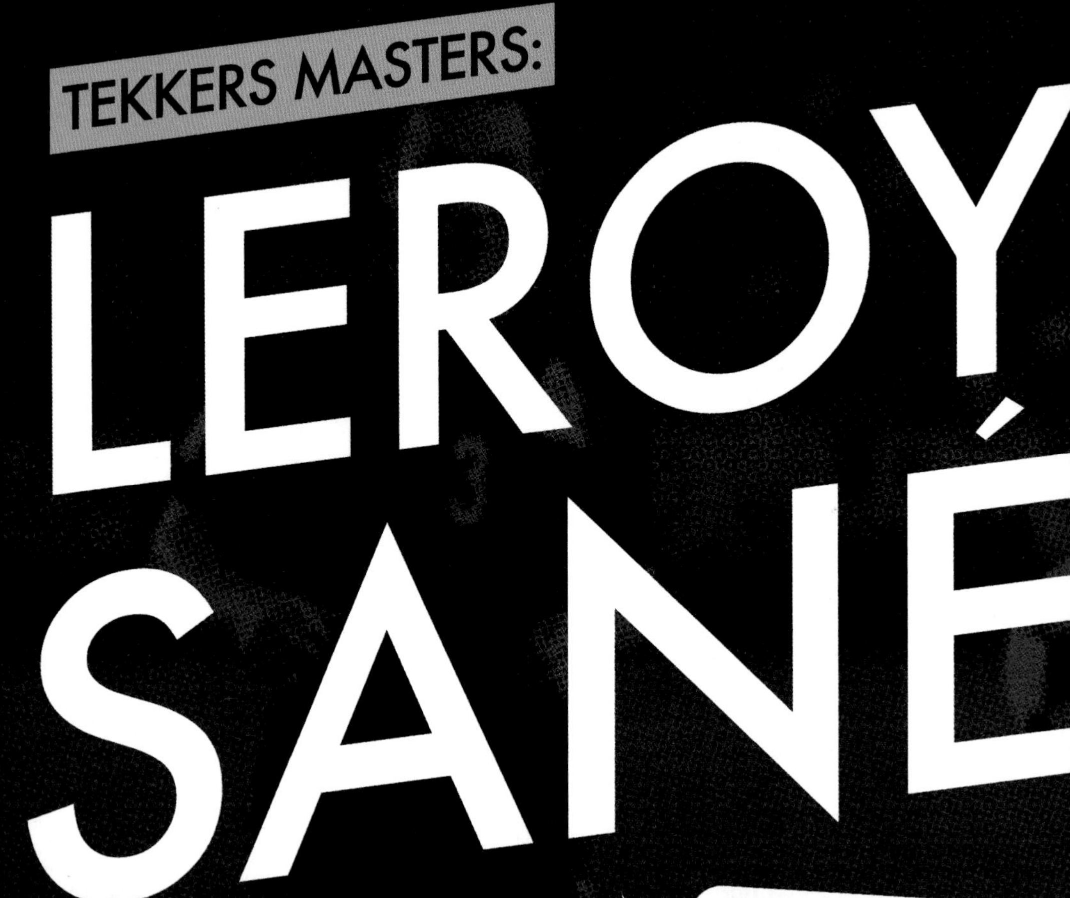

TEKKERS MASTERS:

LEROY SANÉ

'WATCH HIM: HE ALWAYS WANTS TO GO FORWARD'

Jez: Ah, you've got to love a winger, haven't you? And I really like him. He was one of my very favourite players in the Premier League last season. He's just so fast – he's actually incredibly fast. And he can score great goals.

He's got it all really – a good shot, young, immense footballing talent. He's popular among professionals, too. Like, I saw on Danny Simpson's Instagram, where he said Leroy was the best winger this season. He's got quick legs and a quick mind.

Billy: Yeah, people say that his legs are fast, but his brain makes him even sharper. He's also got an incredible build as a footballer. He's quite tall and he's physically strong too.

He's so, so direct. Watch him: he always wants to go forward. He wants to attack, attack, attack. He won't give full-backs a chance when they're up against him. They must be absolutely terrified of him.

That's what the manager wants when he sends out his side – a fast attacker who can scare the opposition. The reason is that if a player is scary to opponents, then he doesn't even have to do anything to make a massively positive impact on a game. Just by his reputation alone he can unsettle the enemy. Anything he does on top just makes him even more lethal.

The other thing is his stamina, which is off the scale. Sané can literally run the whole game. He does not stop. I like the directness of his play. He will attack at every opportunity that he can. He could probably be a striker if he wanted to be.

Jez: I'd actually agree with that. Also, he's got a good attitude. I read that during his teenage years he stepped away from some of what teenage boys generally get up to: partying and so forth. He wanted to focus on his football. I think that's really, really important.

Billy: Oh, totally. This is really essential and one of the most important parts of the book for me. People tell you that you just have to work hard on the training pitch and the field, and they're right.

But no one really tells you that you have to sacrifice and to me this is so important. You get it drummed into you about how hard you have to work on the training ground, that you have to practise, practise, practise.

You might have the technical ability already in place but what no one says is that David Beckham was in bed at 9pm every Friday and Saturday night when he was coming up through the ranks at Old Trafford.

He sacrificed. He could have been out with mates or girls. Doing what everyone else around him would do. He didn't just sacrifice that he sacrificed his whole life.

But he sacrificed it for football – and look at the results!

'SANÉ CAN LITERALLY RUN THE WHOLE GAME.'

Jez: England captain, a treble with Manchester United, played for Real Madrid. Not bad, eh?

Billy: Not bad at all, pal. You can practise all you like and have all the talent but if you don't want to sacrifice, you can't have two separate lives, partying with friends at 17, eating rubbish food, if you want to give yourself a chance, unless you're a one-off true footballing god, you will have to sacrifice things away from football.

Jez: As for Sané, I really think he's established himself now. It took him a short while to find his feet at Manchester City. But then he really got it together around the turn of the year. He's put in some banging performances against Chelsea and Monaco, and I think this is only the beginning for him.

Billy: Yeah, he's going to be speeding up and down pitches for some time. I can't wait to see how he develops.

adidas
19

GET THE SKILLS:

SUÁREZ HEEL FLICK

FACT FILE

ORIGIN: UNKNOWN
SKILL TYPE: DRIBBLE
DIFFICULTY RATING: 8
TEKKERS RATING: 9
FREQUENTLY USED BY: SUÁREZ

Billy: Imagine this: you're out wide on the wing and your team-mate passes the ball to you. The full-back is closing in tight, he might even try to go through the back of you, and suddenly you pull this out. Before he can say Luis Alberto Suárez Díaz, the ball flies over his head and you're off down the line. Hasta la vista, pal!

The delivery is key to this – the ball needs to bounce a couple of feet in front of you, and then you just help it on its way with your heel as you spin and accelerate. Keep your eye on the ball as it comes down over his head, the next touch needs to be spot-on to leave the defender, the defence, hey, the whole world eating your dust.

F2
LET THE BALL BOUNCE IN FRONT
FLICK OUT YOUR HEEL...
...HELP THE BALL OVER...
...THE DEFENDER'S HEAD
ACCELERATE AWAY

DEFENDER CLOSES

LET THE BALL BOUNCE

SPIN AND HEEL FLICK THE BALL...

...OVER THE DEFENDER'S HEAD

ACCELERATE

EYES ON THE BALL
TOUCH!

BILLY V JEZZA

BEST STADIUM

Billy: When we visited the Estádio do Maracanã in Rio de Janeiro, Jez, that was unreal. It has a 78,000 capacity so we were expecting it to be epic but we didn't have a clue until we got there how amazing it is. Took my breath away.

Jez: Yeah it's definitely up there for me, too, but I can't wait to visit the Luzhniki Stadium for this Summers World Cup in Russia. I'm excited about that. I've heard amazing things about it.

Billy: But Jez, I'm going to put this out there: what about the Bernabéu, Real Madrid's stadium, as a winner for this category? You're so high up, not as high at Barca's Camp Nou, but the atmosphere stays in the ground purely because of the roof.

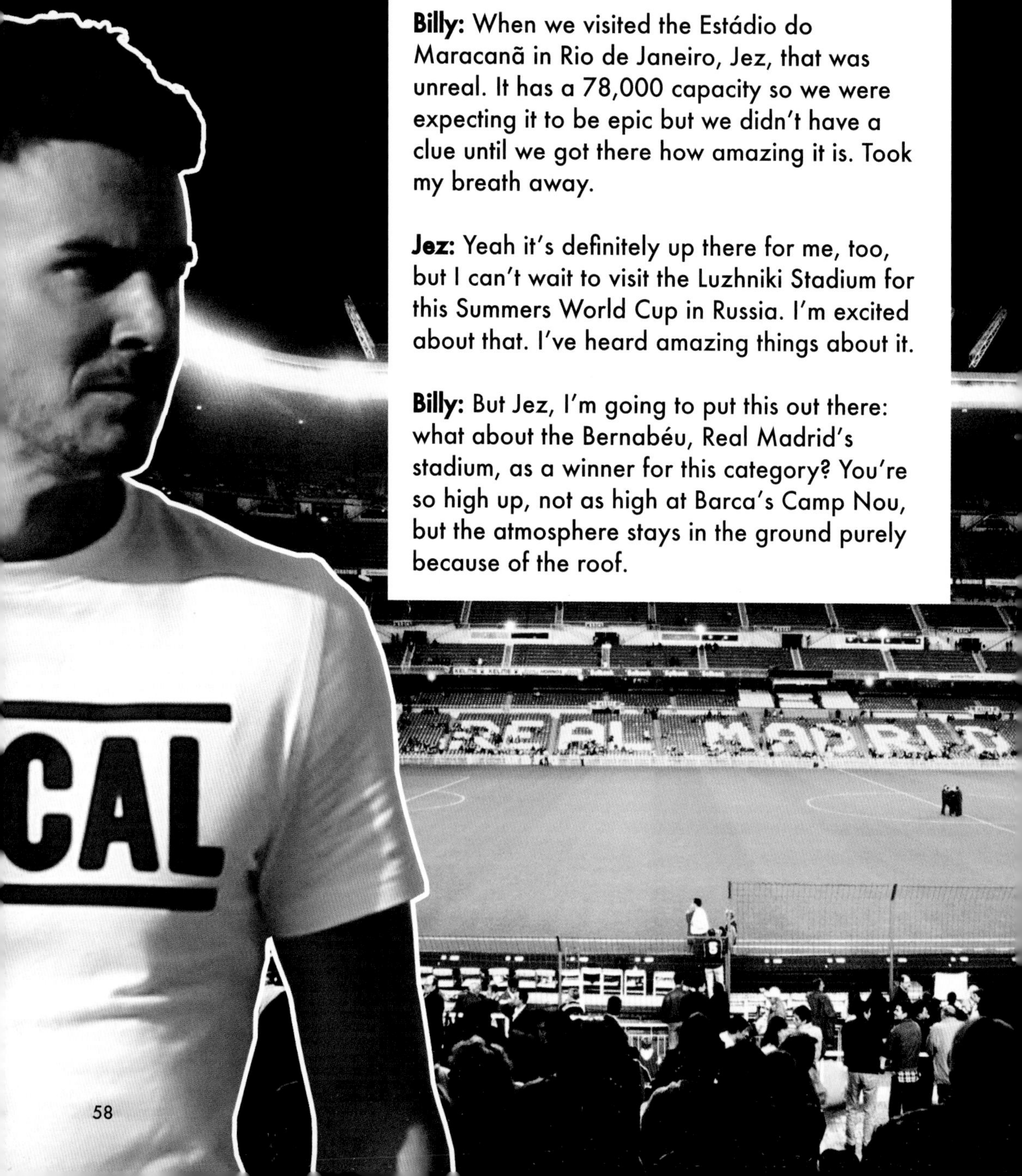

Jez: True, but no: the Camp Nou's got to be the best. We've been there both to watch matches and to film there and come on, it's blown us away. For me, I'm all about the Camp Nou.

Billy: It's a close one, though, isn't it? I wonder what the readers will think...

#TeamBilly: Santiago Bernabéu

#TeamJezza: Camp Nou

You: ______________________

CHAPTER FOUR

F2: WORLD CLASS

PHYSICAL FITNESS

Speed

Jez: If you want to understand the importance of speed in football, you can watch some games from the old, old days on YouTube. Go back to the 1980s, if you really want to find a contrast. What's amazing about then is how much slower the games were. Sometimes, the commentator marvels about the pace of an attacker, but you're sitting there thinking: 'But, but... he's hardly breaking sweat!'

That's because the game is so much more fast and intense now – unbelievably so. Unless you are a goalkeeper, a lot of a match will be split between you sprinting and recovering. It's fast, slow, fast, slow – over and over.

Billy: And a great way of preparing for that intensity is interval training. This means running in a combination of fast pace and slow pace. Here's a simple interval training technique: run for one minute at near your top effort, then run for two minutes at half of your top effort. If you want to take it a step further, as you continue with the pattern, decrease the length of the fast segment but increase the effort.

By the end, you could be absolutely pelting the fast bit!

Jez: Yes, mate. That will really help you replicate the cardio demands of match day. If you really master interval training then next time you're in a match and there's a sudden

change of pace, you'll react much better than anyone. You'll notice a difference.

Billy: Speed's a funny one – it's not just about the speed itself, you need to have the technique to carry it off. Joining a running club will definitely improve your speed and technique. You'll have people watching you and they can help you with your technique. They might notice that you posture is wrong, for instance.

The more you practise, the more you will improve, so technique is important. Even when you're able to run really fast, a new running technique might take you that bit faster, and, as we keep telling you, even the smallest advantage can make all the difference when you want to get to the top level of football.

Strength

Jez: So let's turn to strength. The thing is, strength isn't just about being muscular – it's as much about being clever and knowing how to use your body. Some players are quite small but they're able to use their strength in the best way. They can get that low centre of gravity, which makes it hard to knock them off the ball.

So try to do plenty of core exercises, work on the stability of your core. Your core is made up of the muscles in your torso, especially your abs and your lower back. A lot of strength comes from this area in football. Using your arms goes down to your core, using your legs to try and stabilise yourself goes up to your core.

Billy: People don't always realise how important that central strength is to be powerful on the football pitch. Bulk up your arms if you like, but your core is going to hold opponents off.

Also, working on your core reduces your risk of getting injured because everything goes back to there. The stronger your core is, the less chance you have of a hamstring injury, or any injury.

Jez: To build up your core a lot of what you can do takes place indoors, rather than out in the open air. We all see pictures on Instagram of top players putting in some time in the gym. Some people find the gym a bit boring, and it certainly doesn't offer the adrenaline of smashing the ball in the net, or skinning an opponent on the touchline.

But listen, people, a little bit of gym time goes a long way. A stronger body means you'll be able to tackle better, turn quicker and leap higher for a header. And anyway, don't be worrying so much about being bored. If you love football you won't be bored anyway, you just won't. You'll know that you're putting in the hours for the game.

Importance of repetition

Jez: This mental stamina becomes all the more important when you are trying to get quicker feet. The best way of getting quicker feet is through drills. It's like if you learn the piano. You have to do relentless repetitive practising for your finger exercises. That's how you get there. So it's the same for football. You just have to do drills. That's how you get the muscle memories and that's how you get the speed.

Billy: For faster feet, you could try using mini hurdles. You can devise a simple but massively effective drill with them. Lay five of them out two or three feet apart, depending on your height, and walk up and down, lifting your feet over them. This alone will make your feet quicker and give you the edge over your opponent next time.

Then you can start to jog across them, and when you're confident with that, run along them. But keep an elegant and steady posture – that's how you'll get the most out of it.

Jez: Repetition is the key to success. You know, they did a test on F1 drivers. These guys drive at silly speeds, so they tested their reaction times compared to normal people. In general, their overall reaction times are almost the same, but F1 drivers are so familiar to reacting in a car, their reaction times in cars are so much quicker.

It's the same with anything. By repetition you increase your reaction and speed. That's how it works with quick feet.

Stamina

Billy: Let's go to stamina, we've all seen what players who have great stamina can achieve. Gareth Bale is a prime example of this. He just goes on and on. Footballers cover on average 10 kilometres every game, but people like Bale and Alexis Sanchez often beat the average.

To boost your stamina, try cardiovascular exercise (running, cycling, stair-stepping, jogging, skipping) and keep increasing the increments. Or devise a circuit training routine. This could include sit-ups, push-ups, lunges, squat jumps, and the like.

Jez: Even if you can't use a gym regularly for whatever reason you can build your strength using basic exercises: press-ups, squats and lunges. Swimming is great for football, too. You will build strength, stamina and fitness.

Billy: You often hear football experts say that part of a player's pace is in his head. You could say the same

about stamina, really. For sure, most of your stamina is determined by your body, but you can add that little extra bit in your head. How? By having a positive mental attitude.

Jez: That's right. Once you hit the 70-minute mark in a football match, the psychology goes to a new level. The mentally weaker players will start to think about full-time and putting their feet up. But the stronger ones will drive on, giving it their very best until the last second.

They won't let themselves feel tired or defeated. They will be so strong mentally that they'll chase the game until the final moment. That's a world class attribute. So work on your mental stamina by being positive. If a negative or defeated thought comes into your mind, don't listen to it. Don't even engage it. Notice it has floated into your mind and then notice as it floats away.

It will help your stamina, so keep working on all this. Small margins are the difference between getting to the top and just missing out.

TEKKERS MASTERS:

DAVID DE GEA

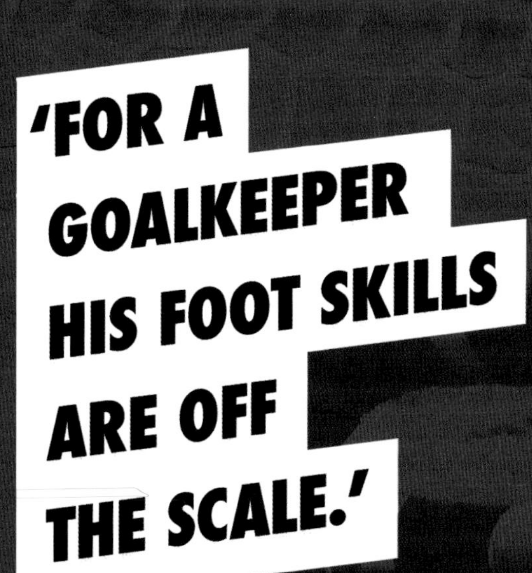

'FOR A GOALKEEPER HIS FOOT SKILLS ARE OFF THE SCALE.'

DAVID DE GEA

SPEED:	9
VISION:	7
TOUCH:	7
SHOT-STOPPING:	10
TEKKERS:	7

F2 TRUMPS

Jez: I think he's the best player in his position at the moment. The amount of qualities this guy has in his locker is amazing.

Billy: Agree about the best in the world. What would you say are his standout skills, Jez?

Jez: Where do I start? He's absolutely amazing with his feet. For a goalkeeper his foot skills are off the scale – on his day he could put some outfield players to shame. He's also probably the best shot-stopper I've ever seen. His positioning is solid and he really commands the penalty area.

Billy: I'm with you on all of that. His instincts and reactions are good, too. You won't get much past him. He's also another one for the big stage; he can conjure up massive saves at key moments.

Jez: And listen, this has a big effect on the defenders. Their mood is shaped a lot by which goalkeeper they've played in front of. I've not played that much in defence, maybe a few times in training to get some perspective. I've always been an attacking player. But I can always see, and feel, the effect that an assured goalkeeper has on his team-mates.

'KEEPERS DON'T ALWAYS GRAB THE HEADLINES BUT DE GEA DOES.'

Billy: That's so true, Jez. Defenders feel better, or worse, depending on the man behind them. One hundered per cent. When I played at semi-pro standard, we had a series of different keepers of different skill levels. Once you have a really good keeper, the difference it makes through the whole team, not just the defence, is unreal.

Why? Because you know that if someone goes one-on-one with your keeper he will have a 50/50 chance. So with De Gea, you know that the opposition has to be at their best to get past him. Look at how many one-on-ones he has saved. He comes out and makes himself as big as possible and its unreal.

Jez: That makes everyone more confident. You feel more motivated to press forward, knowing that there is a decent guy between the sticks. Keepers don't always grab the headlines but De Gea does, because he puts in some simply incredible performances.

Against Arsenal last year he made 14 saves in one match – and many of them were breathtaking. At one stage that season he had kept out an amazing 81.6 per cent of all shots faced. His nearest rival to the top spot was Joe Hart, who was 30 per cent lower. His team-mates have a lot to thank him for.

I think De Gea's physique is interesting too. He's quite slight but also tall - a curious build. But I think it works for him.

Billy: I agree about his build. Not many people are that tall and that thin. I think that allowed him greater speed and better agility. That flexibility is going to be his best chance. I reckon a lot of keepers struggle to have that build. I think it actually helps him.

And with De Gea, the team has the number one player in his position in the world, actually. Not that he has let this billing get the better of him. He was potentially the best keeper in the world a few years ago and he carried on working and improving.

He didn't rest on his laurels. He could have said to himself: 'Manchester United are never going to get rid of me, Real Madrid are

'AGAINST ARSENAL LAST YEAR HE MADE 14 SAVES IN ONE MATCH.'

always going to want me.' But no, he carried on working and has improved. He keeps trying to get better.

Jez: How good could he get? He's 27 as we're writing this book. That's quite young for a goalkeeper as it goes. He's another player who has plenty of confidence in himself. And when we talk about players with confidence in themselves, we don't mean arrogance. We mean a more pure form of confidence. A certain poise and determination; a positivity. He's got all of that in spades. No wonder he keeps improving.

GET THE SKILLS:

ROULETTE PANNA

FACT FILE

ORIGIN: UNKNOWN
SKILL TYPE: DRIBBLE
DIFFICULTY RATING: 9
TEKKERS RATING: 9
FREQUENTLY USED BY:
ZIDANE, BERBATOV, FIRMINO

Billy: Some of you might know the Zidane Turn, sometimes called the Maradona Spin, or the Roulette. That's the cake, but this skill adds a cherry on top. It's a brilliant spinning manoeuvre for getting you out of a tight spot as defenders rush in.

The trick is after you've executed the standard Roulette, you add an extra quick touch with the outside of your weaker foot. The Roulette forces the defender to open their legs to block you and this creates the room for the Panna. Knock it through and sprint round. Piece of cake, really!

AS THE BALL HEADS TO THE TOUCHLINE

STOP THE BALL WITH YOUR STRONG FOOT

JUMP AND ROTATE YOUR BODY

DRAG THE BALL BACK WITH YOUR WEAK FOOT

NUTMEG WITH THE OUTSIDE OF YOUR WEAK BOOT

ACCELERATE AWAY

BILLY V JEZZA

BEST WORLD CUP GOAL

Jez: There are so many we could go through for this one, aren't there? With the planet's greatest players on show at the World Cup, it's no wonder that so many sweet strikes have happened there.

Diego Maradona's second against England at the 1986 World Cup finals is an all-time classic. It's been dubbed the goal of the century and no wonder: he picked up the ball in his own half and set off on a 60-yard run, passing four English outfield players and then leaving the goalkeeper on his backside before slotting the ball home.

Billy: Painful for England but undoubtedly a top, top-class goal.

Jez: And you know, another one we could discuss is the Nelinho goal at the 1978 World Cup finals. Mate, if that's not one of the sweetest slice strikes that I've ever seen in the World Cup I don't know what is. He's just incredible.

But to actually pin my colours to the mast and single one out, this one is easy for me: I'm going to go for Robin van Persie's goal against Spain at the 2014 World Cup finals. *That* header. He just flew at that long pass and nutted it home. Boom! It's simply the best goal I've ever seen in a World Cup. Absolutely incredible skill from the Dutchman.

Billy: Okay, the pressure's on now you've chosen that one. What's mine gonna be? Hmmm, can we use qualifiers?

Jez: It's our book, we can use what we want. Hahaha!

Billy: Simple, then. David Beckham's famous free kick against Greece! He single- handedly dragged us to the World Cup that year and his free kick in the last few minutes was unbelievable.

England were losing 2-1 to Greece when Becks curled home his late goal, sealing a place at the 2002 World Cup. The pressure on him in that moment must have been immense. It was stoppage time but he sent home an unstoppable shot.

That gets my vote!

BECKHAM
BECKHAM
BECKHAM
BECKHAM
BECKHAM

#TeamBilly: **David Beckham,** ENGLAND v Greece, 2001

#TeamJezza: **Robin van Persie,** Spain v HOLLAND, 2014

You: ____________________

QUIPMENT
adidas
ADV / 91-17

F2 CHAPTER FIVE

F2: WORLD CLASS

DEVELOPING SKILL

Billy: Jez, tell me something. If you want to get twice as good as you are at football, what is a superfast way to double your skill level?

Jez: The clue is in the word football – you get better by working on both of your feet. I mean, look, there are some naturally two-footed players around, but for a lot of us we have one stronger foot. So you have to work on your weaker foot. Your game will improve so much.

There are really easy ways of practising this. Go down the park with a mate and ping the ball back and forward between each other, but each of you using your weaker foot. Then, to take it a step further, when you are practising specific skills, try doing some of them with your weaker foot.

Billy: That sounds quite a... feat, Jez. Geddit?

Jez: I'm going to choose to ignore that remark. But this sort of training is something that Dennis Bergkamp was big on. When one of the Premier League's greatest ever stars says something, you know you need to listen. The guy was a magician.

Billy: He was, and speaking of the Dutch, I know that in Holland they get kids doing a series of quick touches in unison in sets of 100–200 repetitions. That might sound like a lot, but there

are theories that it takes 10,000 hours of practice to master any skill in life. If that sounds like too long, then at least try and get yourself near it. How about 10,000 touches of the football?

That would be a lot but I'm going to put this out there: you guys reading this, you can do more touches than you are at the moment. I'm confident that's the case. Up the numbers a bit. Really get your cushioning perfected.

Jez: Here's a great way of really developing your skill: creating match scenarios when you practise. You shouldn't see match days and training days as entirely different things. Training is there to prepare you for a match, but it should also reflect a match.

So if there's quite a few of you, you can break into two groups and then rehearse scenarios. One group can surge at the other group, then you get practice at defending and attacking all in one moment. Bring some edge and competitiveness to training.

Billy: When I read interviews with some of the top players from legendary teams, they often talk about how competitive things got during training. Now part of that is down to hunger, for sure. But it's also because world-class players understand that you'll only excel on the pitch if you have tested yourself on the training field.

I've read that in some of Sir Alex Ferguson's trophy winning teams and the Invincibles of Arsenal, they would be sliding in on each other in training. One time, Kolo Touré even took out Arsène Wenger! I'm not recommending that sort of thing exactly, but I'm saying you need to take training seriously. Don't be the guy who is too cool to give it some because it's 'just' practising.

The rondo is a great practice to bring this out. It's a bit like a footballing piggy-in-the-middle, where a larger group of players has the ball and a smaller number of players tries to win it back. The top academies at Barcelona and Ajax have made this a staple of their training.

Jez: Yeah and Johan Cruyff (a Dutch Tekkers Master from the 1970s) said: 'Everything that goes on in a match, except shooting, you can do in a rondo.' So it's definitely one for your training.

You can do it in a number of different variants: 3 versus 1; 4 versus 1; 5 versus 2 and upwards. Change the amount of touches the possessing team is allowed based on the skill level or age of the guys. Find a way that works for you.

But remember: keep it intense. You can't muck about all week and then expect to be the best on Saturday. Your match-day experience will reflect your training approach. Even if there's not a big group of you practising, you can benefit by just doing it with one mate who you really trust, because you can ping each other feedback.

Billy: Looking up is a big part of any skill and one that a mate can easily help you out with. It's easy to fall into the trap of looking down at your feet all the time – because that's where you want most of the magic to happen. But you won't do well if you're not looking up a lot, so ask your mates to shout at you if they catch you looking down too much. Do the same for them!

Jez: That's right, Bill.

Billy: And even if there are days when your mates are busy and you have to train on your tod in the garden, there are ways to make it easier. Surround yourself with cushions, so when you mess up a skill, you don't need to keep chasing after the ball.

And when you are learning a skill, break it down into its separate parts first. Then just master the first part. Don't move on to the second until you've got the first one sorted. Master the parts bit by bit. The reason for this is that you might feel overwhelmed if you try and do it all at once.

So many times, players who could have improved end up standing still because they tried to take on too much at once, rather than developing their skills bit by bit.

Jez: So true. Get yourself a routine that you can practise every day. Do it so many times that it is drilled into your mind and body. We can all be impatient and you might want results faster than in 10,000 hours' time. But you will only get out of training what you put into it.

TEKKERS MASTERS:

ANTOINE GRIEZMANN

'HE'S ACTUALLY EXTREMELY TECHNICALLY GIFTED. HE'S ALSO REALLY BRIGHT, HE'S GOT SUPER HIGH FOOTBALL INTELLIGENCE.'

Jez: He's definitely one of the best players in the world – I like him a lot. And I tell you, something that isn't said enough about players like Griezmann is that he works so very hard. He's got a great attitude and a great work rate.

He's actually extremely technically gifted. He's also really bright, he's got super-high football intelligence. How I'd put it is that he reads the game well. This means he is able to predict and pre-empt what's going to happen before it happens. All the best players in the world can anticipate this way.

Billy: Yeah, he definitely reads the game well. If you're reading this and you want to master this attribute, here's how. Firstly, you have to understand the game and the players around you in the team and where they fit in.

Then, you need to understand each other. So you know when the other players will make their runs, where they will go, when to release the ball to them.

When I was delivering crosses I would know where and when to release the ball. I would look up and think 'I know he wants to dart near post' because of his body language, or because we're just on the same wavelength. I think this is really important: understanding your team-mates and where they like to receive the ball.

Jez: It's almost eerie sometimes when you see it in action, you know? You think: how did he know that was about to happen?

I mean, look, you can never really know for sure. Football is a random game. But players like Antoine can very quickly calculate probabilities in their mind. They won't always be right, but it will go for them more often than it will go against them. It all comes with experience. Some players do it naturally but it can be learned too.

Billy: It's like you paint a picture. I've heard so many top players describe the game that way – they paint a picture in their minds.

So you're looking at the game around you and you can see what is going to happen next. For instance, if I make a run from the wing and cut in for a through ball, I'm already visualising that through ball coming and what I'm going to do next. I might be thinking: I'm quite wide here, but I can see the striker in the centre and I'm looking to whip it into him straight away.

The guy who plays the through ball is already on my wavelength. The striker knows that I'm too far out to shoot, so he's making the run to receive my pass before I've even got the ball myself.

Jez: Griezmann's a threat every time he takes to the field. His finishing is superb and so is his all-round play. His technique and vision are amazing. He can drop deep and link-up play between the attackers and the midfield. He can play as a main striker, as a central attacking midfielder or as a wide man. For such a small guy he's also dangerous in the air. What a package.

He's superb, and I think that at many points over the last few years he has been the greatest player in Europe.

I read that he says he models his game on David Silva and David Beckham. And now, kids are modelling their game on Antoine Griezmann. He's definitely one to learn from, readers!

Billy: And, like all footballers, this guy has had some knocks and some setbacks. Don't think for a moment that everything goes his way. He was told he was too small to make it as a pro when he was growing up in France and he had to move to Spain before he was given a proper chance. He's had days and even weeks where things won't work for him, where some people would have given up. But he didn't give up. He kept trying. When he fell over, he picked himself up, dusted himself down and got on with it. And then, at Euro 2016, he's top scorer and named Player of the Tournament.

That's why when you see these Tekkers Masters succeed, whether

'HIS FINISHING IS SUPERB AND SO IS HIS ALL ROUND PLAY.'

that's scoring a goal or grabbing a win or a trophy, you can't help but be delighted for them. Because you know that they are human beings who just want to be the best they can. And as we've said, that's what we want for everyone in the F2 family. We want everyone to be the very best they can.

GET THE SKILLS:

TRIPLE ELASTICO

FACT FILE

ORIGIN: UNKNOWN
SKILL TYPE: DRIBBLE
DIFFICULTY RATING: 9
TEKKERS RATING: 9
FREQUENTLY USED BY:
DAVIDS, RONALDINHO

Jez: What's better than an Elastico? A Double Elastico? How about a Triple Elastico! Is he going left? No he's going right, no he's going left. Boom! This one's going to leave your defender with his legs in a tangle and his brain in a wrangle. It's a flap-flip-flap.

To supersize your Elastico, start with your legs wide. Tap the ball across your body with your instep. Stop it with the outside of the same boot before executing the standard elastic – push the ball back across your body with the outside of your boot and then instantly switch back again to the instep. Start slowly and speed up with practice. Work off both feet to be truly World Class.

F2
SPREAD YOUR LEGS
TOUCH WITH YOUR INSTEP
SHIFT TO OUTSTEP...
...AND QUICKLY BACK TO INSTEP
PUSH OFF AND ACCELERATE

SPREAD...

INSTEP ACROSS YOUR BODY

OUTSTEP, AND IN ONE MOTION...

...INSTEP AGAIN

PUSH OFF
RESPECT
AND ACCELERATE

BILLY V JEZZA

BEST WORLD CUP SKILLS

Billy: Let's get the ball rolling on this one with James Rodríguez's moment against Uruguay in 2014. That chest control and swivelled volley was an incredible piece of skill. If you haven't heard the Colombian commentary of that goal then take a look on YouTube. It's unreal!

Jez: Okay, but what about Dennis Bergkamp's touch and goal versus Argentina in 1998 though Bill? That was pretty special, too. An iconic moment from the Iceman. With a minute or so to go, he took those three magnificent touches and scored the winner against Argentina that put Holland into the World Cup semi-final.

Billy: Wow, I remember it Jez, but if we're talking skill...what about Blanco in 1998 against South Korea, we'd never seen that move before. They call it the bunny hop: if you're facing two defenders, lock the ball between your feet and jump past them. To make it work, you need to really get away quickly though!

Jez: It's audacious to say the least! Even though it was a friendly, I want to also mention the scorpion kick from René Higuita. That moment when he dived forward and flicked up both of his heels to clear the ball was amazing. He actually looked like a scorpion!

#TeamBilly: James Rodríguez,
Chest control and volley, COLUMBIA v Uruguay, 2014

#TeamJezza: Dennis Bergkamp,
Touch, turn and strike, HOLLAND v Argentina, 1998

You: ____________________

HALF-TIME: ACTIVITIES

Billy: Work hard, play hard, that's the trick. You've nailed the first half of the book and now it's time for a well-earned break.

Call it recovery time.

Jez: That's right. Being World Class isn't just about training your feet, it's also about training your brain. Here are some fun activities to quicken your mind. Remember the first few yards are always in your head. Good luck!

HALF-TIME:

SPOT THE BALL

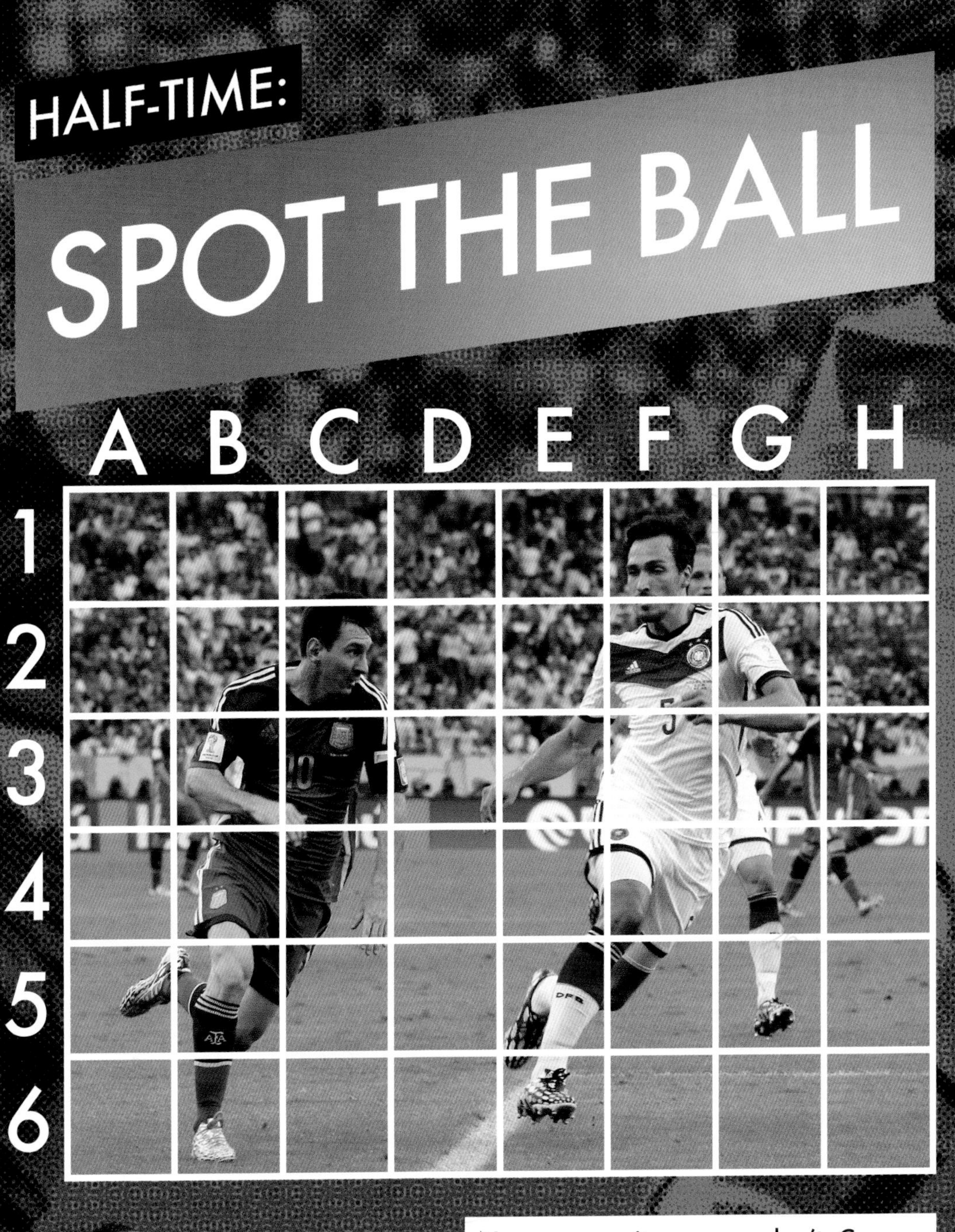

Now you see it, now you don't. Can you understand where the ball is just by body-shape alone? The top stars can. Have a go.

Answer in the back

HALF-TIME:

SPOT THE DIFFERENCE

Spot all 6!

Answers in the back

HALF-TIME:

WORD SEARCH

Answers in the back

Can you find these ten tekkers words hidden in this wordsearch? You will need the sort of vision that a playmaker like Mesut Özil uses when he seeks out his teammates on a crowded field.

K A N E R I Z E T R D K E E L
S H D F O X S Z L P R M C L S
D D H C N Y L S E A T A A P M
T M G Q A M B I E G S B E G C
O V A Q L P Y F E M E T P N T
E O R D D X E V R L S O I C P
C C T E O B O Q K Z X R O C E
X P O L N L L C C R N T H Z O
K X O D Z I U F W T D B N M Z
Q Q U F X N O F E N J G G Q U
B Y G U K O A K L B K W F L O
V G N S D E K N B P Q Z E R D
L I D Q Q E S J W J L O L P H
W I N G R O V E Q M P Y V P N
O C U S E G G V Z I W W I E X

Ronaldo | Wingrove | Lynch | Love | Tekkers
Knuckleball | Elastico | Messi | Peace | Kane

HALF-TIME:

IT'S THE F2 QUIZ!

We've loved sharing our journey with the rest of the F2 family. Now, we want to know if you have been paying attention. Here's 20 questions about us which will separate the F2 fans from the F2 fanatics. Good luck, guys!

1. WHICH OF US GREW UP IN ENFIELD: BILL OR JEZ?
2. WHAT WAS THE NAME OF THE FOOTBALL DOCUMENTARY JEZ STARRED IN BEFORE HIS F2 DAYS?
3. ONE OF US HAS A COUSIN, GREG, WHO TURNED OUT FOR ENGLAND SCHOOLBOYS.
4. WHICH REALITY TELEVISION SERIES DID JEZ ENTER?
5. TRUE OR FALSE: BILLY SPENT A PERIOD ON LOAN AT ITALIAN SIDE TORINO
6. WHAT WAS THE NAME OF THE TELEVISION SERIES WE FILMED IN LOS ANGELES IN 2017?
7. WHICH F1 LEGEND'S YACHT DID WE PARTY ON WHEN WE WENT TO MONACO?
8. JEZ GOT AN INJURY TO WHICH PART OF HIS FOOT IN 2017: HIS ANKLE OR HEEL?
9. WHAT IS BILL'S SURNAME?

10. AND WHAT IS JEZ'S SECOND NAME?

11. WHAT WAS THE TITLE OF OUR FIRST BOOK?

12. THE FIRST FOOTBALL MATCH BILL ATTENDED AS A KID WAS BETWEEN COVENTRY AND WHICH OTHER SIDE?

13. WHICH POP LEGEND DID WE STUDY TO PUT TOGETHER ONE OF OUR EARLIEST ROUTINES: ED SHEERAN OR MICHAEL JACKSON?

14. WHICH IS THE NAME OF OUR CLOTHING BRAND?

15. WHICH OF US TOOK AN IQ TEST AND GOT A GENIUS SCORE OF 161?

16. WHICH YOUTUBER FILMED AND PRODUCED OUR CONTENT FOR SEVERAL YEARS?

17. IN WHICH YEAR DID WE FORM THE F2?

18. WHICH AWARD DID WE WIN IN 2012?

19. NAME THE SPANISH GIANT CLUB WE TRAINED WITH IN 2016?

20. FINALLY, NAME THE FOOTBALL CEREMONY WE PERFORMED AT IN 2010?

HOW DID YOU DO? A RATINGS GUIDE!

Answers in the back

0-5 CORRECT: It's back to school for you, son.
5-10 CORRECT: You're a promising talent, making your way up the ranks. Keep plugging away!
10-15 CORRECT: A quality performance. Pat yourself on the back and bask in the acclaim of the fans.
15-19 CORRECT: Wow, you are officially a Tekkers Master. It doesn't get much better than this...
20 CORRECT: ...except for this. You are the Leo Messi of the mind. Swaz!

Your next challenge, if you choose to accept it, is to complete the F2 Crossword. We're putting you to the test here, guys, and if you've been paying attention to our videos and books, as well as the beautiful game itself, you'll be at a proper advantage.

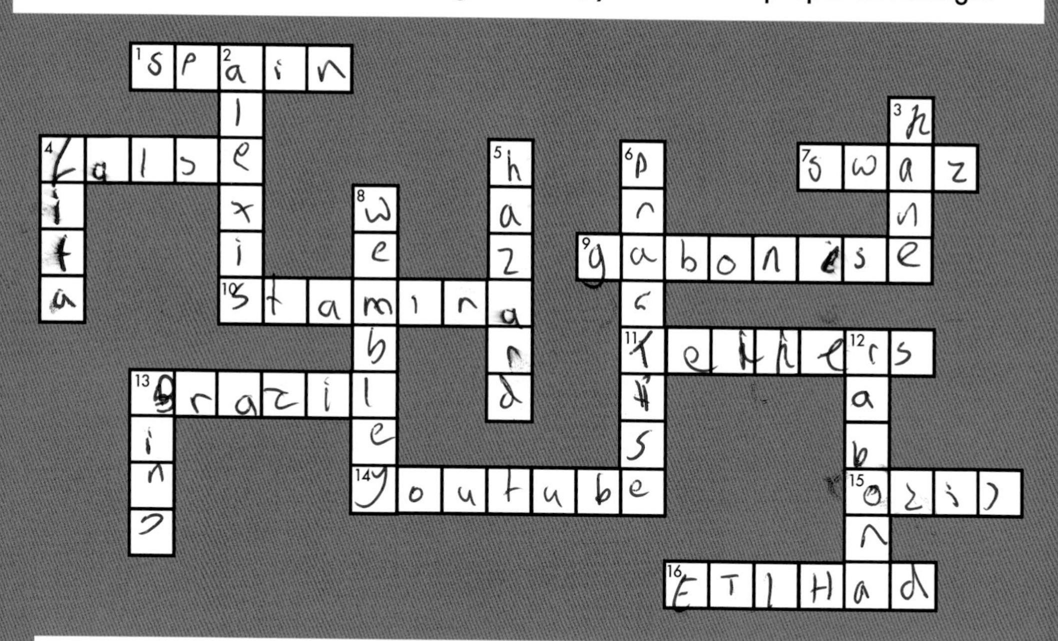

ACROSS

1. This nation won the 2010 World Cup without losing a game
4. A decoy centre forward is known as a _____ 9
7. When you put a bend on the ball...or do anything cool
9. What nationality is Pierre-Emerick Aubameyang?
10. You'll need this to be at your best throughout a game
11. Our catchphrase is Love, Peace and...
13. The nation that has won a record five World Cups
14. The channel that hosts our videos
15. This Arsenal tekkers master won the World Cup with Germany in 2014
16. Manchester City play at the _____ Stadium

DOWN

2. This Chilean moved from Arsenal to Manchester United
3. The striker destined to lead England in the World Cup
4. Football's governing body which holds the World Cup
5. This Chelsea playmaker has a dangerous surname
6. Put in plenty of this to be world class
8. This stadium hosted the 1966 World Cup Final
12. The Argentinian skill where you whip your striking leg round the back of your standing leg
13. The top corner of the goal is also known as Top _____

Answers in the back

HALF-TIME: WORLD CUP QUIZ

Answers in the back

1. How many times have 2014 winners Germany lifted the World Cup?
2. How many teams take part in World Cup final tournaments?
3. What is the Adidas Golden Boot awarded for?
4. Why were the World Cup tournaments cancelled in 1942 and 1946?
5. Which Brazilian legend won the World Cup in 1958, 1962 and 1970?
6. In which year did England win the World Cup?
7. True or false: Brazil used to play in a white kit.
8. When was the first World Cup held: 1930, or 1888?
9. Two nations hosted the World Cup in 2002: Korea and which other?
10. What is the World Cup trophy's name?
11. What creature was Fuleco, the mascot for the 2014 World Cup?
12. True or false: Uruguay have never won a World Cup
13. Which team lost 7-1 to Germany at the 2014 World Cup?
14. And who was the top scorer in the same tournament: James Rodríguez or Lukas Podolski?
15. Which nation hosted the 2010 World Cup finals?
16. Name the top scorer at that tournament
17. Which Tekkers Master was the England captain at the 2014 World Cup: Frank Lampard or Steven Gerrard?
18. And who was the gaffer for the Three Lions in the same tournament?
19. Bora Milutinović has managed five different countries at World Cup finals. Name any one of them.
20. How many World Cups has England qualified for, including the 2018 tournament?

HALF-TIME: STATS 'N' FACTS

Of 204 penalties taken in World Cup shootouts, 162 were right-footed and 42 left-footed.

171

The 2014 World Cup saw a joint-high number of goals scored.

Ronaldo is Brazil's top scorer at World Cups with 15 goals in 4 tournaments.

5

Mexico's Antonio Carbajal and Lothar Matthaüs of Germany have played at the most World Cup tournaments: five in total.

21st

2018 will be the 21st World Cup, 88 years after the initial tournament in Uruguay.

7-1

Germany's 7-1 win in 2014 was the biggest margin of victory ever seen in a World Cup semi-final.

7-5

Austria and Switzerland shared a record 12 goals in the 1954 quarter-final. The match ended 7-5 to Austria!

Paul Pogba was named the young player of the 2014 World Cup.

ONE BILLION

More than one billion fans tuned in to watch the final of the 2014 FIFA World Cup.

Cristiano Ronaldo has scored seven goals at World Cup finals.

Sandor Kocsis of Hungary was the top scorer at the 1954 World Cup – he netted 11 times.

A walloping 13 goals were netted by Just Fontaine of France at the 1958 finals.

THEY SAID IT...

'YOU HAVE TO FIGHT TO REACH YOUR DREAM. YOU HAVE TO SACRIFICE AND WORK HARD FOR IT.' LIONEL MESSI

'SUCCESS IS NO ACCIDENT. IT IS HARD WORK, PERSEVERANCE, LEARNING, STUDYING, SACRIFICE AND MOST OF ALL, LOVE OF WHAT YOU ARE DOING OR LEARNING TO DO.' PELÉ

'THERE IS NO HARM IN DREAMING OF BECOMING THE WORLD'S BEST PLAYER. IT IS ALL ABOUT TRYING TO BE THE BEST.' CRISTIANO RONALDO

'GIVING UP IS NOT AN OPTION' ZLATAN IBRAHIMOVIC

'WHEN TIMES ARE DOWN, KEEP BELIEVING, KEEP WORKING HARD, AND THINGS WILL PICK UP.' HARRY KANE

'THE F2 ARE GENIUS.' JOE HART

'THE F2 ARE THE FUTURE.' STEVEN GERRARD

'THE F2 ARE PHENOMENAL.' NEYMAR

'HOW ARE THE F2 NOT PLAYING IN THE PREMIER LEAGUE?' DELE ALLI

'THE F2 ARE UNBELIEVABLE – WHAT THEY DO IS NOT POSSIBLE!' PELÉ

F2
CHAPTER
SIX

F2: WORLD CLASS

RECOVERY

Jez: When you're training to become a footballer, the hardest times can sometimes be the times when you have to do nothing. You can't be running around 24/7. Even Alexis Sanchez knows you have to rest from time to time!

Billy: This is so true, Jez. There will be some days when the very best thing you can to do improve your game is a very simple thing: nothing. When you're really committed, when making it is the most important thing to you, it can be hard to let up. But there's very good reasons not to overdo it.

Jez: And one of them is what happens if you go too far. We've all heard of training, but have you heard of overtraining? It's a thing, you know? So if you're suffering from constant soreness in your muscles, or you keep feeling ill and become easily exhausted, or if you can't sleep and feel irritable, these can all be signs that you've overdone it.

Billy: As if these symptoms aren't bad enough on their own, if you are overtraining you are also putting yourself in increased danger of picking up injuries. You simply can't be 'on it' every day. Your body won't let you, and that's why you need to rest. It's not just your body, it's also your mind. Mentally, you cannot concentrate all the time. You need to rest your body and mind, so they are at 100 per cent in the big moments.

The top players in the world know this, so do the coaching staff at all the top clubs. That's why, after a World Cup or European Championships, the players who took part in those tournaments usually return to pre-season training later, and at a more gradual pace. If their clubs threw them in regardless, they'd be breaking down with injuries or fatigue by mid-September!

So they ease them in at a different rate to the players who had their feet up on the beach all summer.

Jez: Here's how you go about recovering like a pro. Let's start with sleep. Seriously, guys, if you don't sleep properly, you're wasting the rest of your effort. Loads of clubs, including Real Madrid and both the Manchester sides, have called in sleep coaches to inform their players of how important it is to kip.

And I read about a study in America that showed basketball players who increased their sleep duration to up to 10 hours improved their shot accuracy by 9 per cent and improved their sprint and reaction times.

Billy: Like with a lot of things, the perfect amount of sleep you should have varies from individual to individual. A lot of experts seem to agree that seven or eight hours a night is around the average to aim for. But a lot will add that an afternoon nap can do a lot for your game, too. In Spain they

have siestas, so that's an example to follow!

Jez: Bill, do you remember Michael Essien who played for Chelsea a few years back? He said he slept for 14 hours a night so he could be calm enough and full of energy for matches.

And it worked. For those who don't remember him, he was an energetic, box-to-box midfielder. He was like the Kanté of his day. He got up and down the pitch all afternoon. So you can see how sleep works. Get good-quality kip: that means avoiding sugary drinks or caffeine before you turn in.

Billy: There are other things you can do to aid recovery. A lot of top runners and cyclists have ice baths. They will help you get rid of aches and pains in the short term. You don't need to go all the way to the ice bath, though. Even just 10 minutes in cold water will make a difference.

Jez: You can also use foam rollers to help remove tension from your muscles. Physios, osteopaths and coaches swear by them.

Billy: To sum all this up, just remember that you need to peak at the right moment. Proper recovery is the key to that.

TEKKERS MASTERS:

SERGIO RAMOS

'I WOULDN'T WANT TO PLAY AGAINST HIM.'

Jez: He's a controversial guy but we think he's great. We'd love to film with him. He's such a leader, such a leader. Just look at the goals he scores. So often they come in situations where Real needed their skipper to lead by example. He battles in every game until all hope is gone, he doesn't understand the concept of giving something up as a lost cause. What a character!

Billy: You spotted him early, didn't you, Jez?

Jez: I did. You know, in Texas there's something called the Dallas Cup. When I was there to film the Diego Maradona film, there was a match between Manchester United and Real Madrid sides. It was an under 23, or a youth cup, or something of that sort.

Anyway, I remember watching Sergio Ramos in that game. He was so young but I looked at him and thought he's going to go on to amazing things. And he has – he's gone on to be Sergio Ramos!

Billy: Not a bad thing to become, is it? He's a defender who scores goals. Like you said, Jez, how many important goals has this guy scored? He's a match-winner.

He can really play. He's not a traditional centre-back who is just a typical bully and can't play. I'm sure if he went to a centre-midfield holding role he could smash it. He's a ball player.

I realise some people don't like him but he is a player who you can see plays with ultimate passion. You can see the passion flowing through him and defining his every move. I have so much admiration for that guy.

He gets booked and sent off a lot because it means so much to him. I don't mind that. I think managers don't mind it so much either. Because it shows how much he cares about winning.

Jez: Even in the tunnel before games he will be taking a real lead and laying the groundwork for victory. He'll even be going up to Cristiano Ronaldo and slapping him in the face, saying 'come on, mate'. You can tell that Ronaldo looks up to him as a leader. There's not many players in the world who Ronaldo would look up to and accept as a leader in his team. There's not many players who would have the guts to treat Ronaldo that way.

I just think Ramos is a supreme alpha male – and that comes across in how he plays. Sure, he gets a lot of cards but that's exciting, man. And I tell you what: I wouldn't want to play against him. For opponents he must be really intimidating. Isn't that what it all comes down to? Everyone should aim to be the player who opponents prefer not to face. That's just basic, right?

'HIS DESIRE TO WIN FLOWS THROUGH HIS VEINS.'

Billy: I think that Ramos is another of those players who doesn't just see the game as a job, as the way he earns his salary. No, he sees it as his life, his passion. It's like his desire to win flows through his veins.

Jez: And he has been a winner to end all winners. He's won 18, count them, 18 major honours. As I'm writing this, these include four La Liga titles and three Uefa Champions League titles. That's just for his club! He's also won the World Cup and two Euros.

Billy: And let's not get started on all the individual honours this guy has got on his sideboard. He's a medal magnet!

Jez: Haha, yeah, he has won so much during his career and yet when you watch him, each season he's still pushing himself so hard. There's never that moment where he stands still and says: I've made it.

Billy: No, those words don't seem to be in his vocabulary. He's more the type who says to himself: what could I have done better? How can I improve?

Jez: Yeah, he's one of those players. And you know what those players are called?

Billy: World class players!

GET THE SKILLS:

WINGROVE SIDE SLING

FACT FILE

ORIGIN: NEW EXCLUSIVE SKILL!
INVENTED BY BILLY WINGROVE, UK
SKILL TYPE: DRIBBLE
DIFFICULTY RATING: 10
TEKKERS RATING: 10
FREQUENTLY USED BY:
MR B. WINGROVE

Billy: Here's a brand new one. If this skill had a Nando's Peri-Peri chilli rating, it would be extra, extra hot. Don't be bringing your mild talent to this bad-boy, because this one's fiery. It's got a touch of the F2 Akka (See *World of Football*), but with a brand new starting point.

Break the skill down into two separate parts: practise the knee-touch and toe-hook together by just throwing the ball to yourself. Once you've mastered that, you can add in the back-heel flick-up. It's not easy, but then again it does come with a warning: if your opposition plays with fire they're going to get burned.

APPROACH DEFENDER
RESPECT
FLICK UP USING YOUR HEEL...
...AND INSTEP

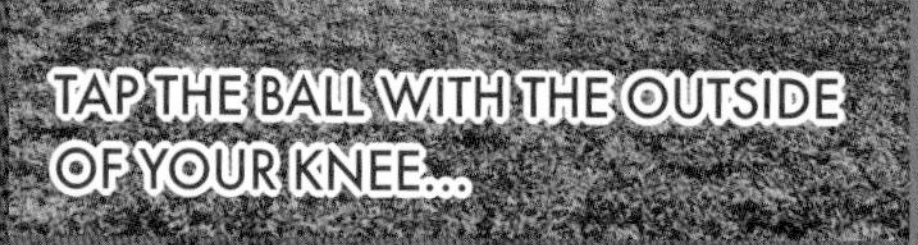

TAP THE BALL WITH THE OUTSIDE OF YOUR KNEE...

QUICKLY HOOK IT WITH YOUR TOE...

...PAST THE DEFENDER

RACE ROUND THE OTHER SIDE

GET ON YOUR BIKE!

BILLY V JEZZA

BEST WORLD CUP CELEBRATIONS

Billy: Oh, there's been some crazy dance moves over the years Jez, hasn't there?

Jez: Mate some celebrations are like watching you on the dance floor!

Billy: Hahaha, me and Roger Milla have got some serious moves!

Jez: I'm going for Bebeto and Brazil's 'rocking baby' celebration from the 1994 World Cup. It was brilliant: Bebeto cradled an imaginary baby alongside his team-mates Romário and Mazinho to celebrate a goal in the 3-2 quarter-final victory over Holland.

Billy: Nice, I'm going for Peter Crouch's robot! I remember when he pulled it out of the bag in a friendly against Jamaica shortly before the 2006 World Cup.

Jez: And what about that Italian player in the eighties who just loses it completely? Marco Tardelli. He just sprints away screaming and waving his arms like a mad person. Imagine that feeling...

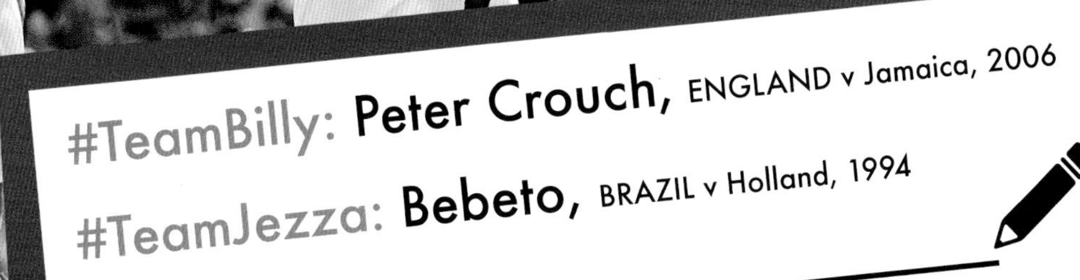
#TeamBilly: Peter Crouch, ENGLAND v Jamaica, 2006
#TeamJezza: Bebeto, BRAZIL v Holland, 1994
You: ____________________

F2 CHAPTER SEVEN

F2: WORLD CLASS NUTRITION

Billy: If you want to get the maximum out of your body, you have to really pay attention to what you're putting in to your body.

Jez: That's right, Bill. Look at the elite players like Alexis Sanchez and Cristiano Ronaldo and you can see that these guys are really careful about what they eat and drink. You can see it: their pace and stamina are top notch, and their physique is frighteningly athletic. They're not mucking about with junk food or unhealthy drinks.

Billy: We spoke to our friend Simon White, who is an experienced sports nutritionist. He told us his golden rule: 'You can't out-train a bad diet.'

Jez: That's so true. You can train really well but if you don't eat the right things then you're basically chucking all that effort straight down the plughole.

But listen, this doesn't mean that nutrition is more important than training. You can't just eat the right things, give training a miss and become a world-class footballer. So come at it from a different perspective: nutrition and training fit together like two best mates. Handle them both right and they'll bring the best out in each other.

Billy: We realise that it can be hard to get the nutrition side right. The thing is, junk food and unhealthy drinks can be tempting, especially after you've played or trained hard. So people make bad choices all the time – even people who are pretty serious about their sport. So as Simon told us, eating a balanced diet will really give you the edge.

Jez: People talk a lot about a balanced diet, but what does it actually mean? Simon said there are three main components: carbohydrates, protein and fat.

You can get carbohydrates from foods like pasta and rice. Oats are also a good source of carbohydrates, so porridge is an excellent breakfast choice.

Plenty of protein is so important, especially when you're a young athlete and your body is still growing. Simon recomended poultry as a good source – chicken in particular. He said you can also get protein from beef, fish and eggs.

Billy: We asked Simon about fat, too. It sounds like an area you could easily get wrong and end up carrying a bit of the old timber! He said you should aim for a balance of healthy fats – both monounsaturated and polyunsaturated. A good source of healthy fat comes by simply cooking with olive oil. Eggs have good fats and nuts are excellent too.

Jez: So: good carbs for energy, good protein for muscle replenishment and muscle building, then fats, vitamins and minerals for a healthy lifestyle. Right there you've got a dietary 'front three'. You're already on to a winner.

Billy: Don't be fooled by fancy labels, either. Simon's advice is that if you are under 16 then give the supplements and protein shakes a miss. Just don't touch them for now.

Jez: Although nutrition is different from person to person, there are some basic rules that should work for everyone. Your pre-match fuel should be higher on carbs and lower on fat. Simon's got a quick bit of maths for you, the meal should be: 60 per cent carbs, 30 per cent protein, 10 per cent fat.

Billy: And then after the game you can have some carbs but there has to be protein post game. You can have fats as well. And remember the golden rule: you cannot out-train a bad diet.

SIMON'S TOP TIPS

1 Eat a balanced diet. You'd be surprised how many people focus really hard on getting their training regime right but then waste all that effort by eating an unhealthy diet.

2 Timing is important. Just like a striker times his runs into the box so he can collect the pass from his team-mate, you've got to time when you eat and drink so you get the most out of it.

On match day, eat two hours before a game ideally. Then, in the first hour after the game, your body is the most efficient at using any energy you consume. After that hour it becomes less and less efficient. So make sure you use that window to get good carbs and lots of protein to repair your muscles and then plenty of rest.

3 It's important to give yourself a treat from time to time. So if you've worked hard on your game all week feel free to have a pizza or a burger on a Saturday night. You can make it healthier by creating your own pizza or burger at home rather than going to a fast-food chain and eating one of theirs.

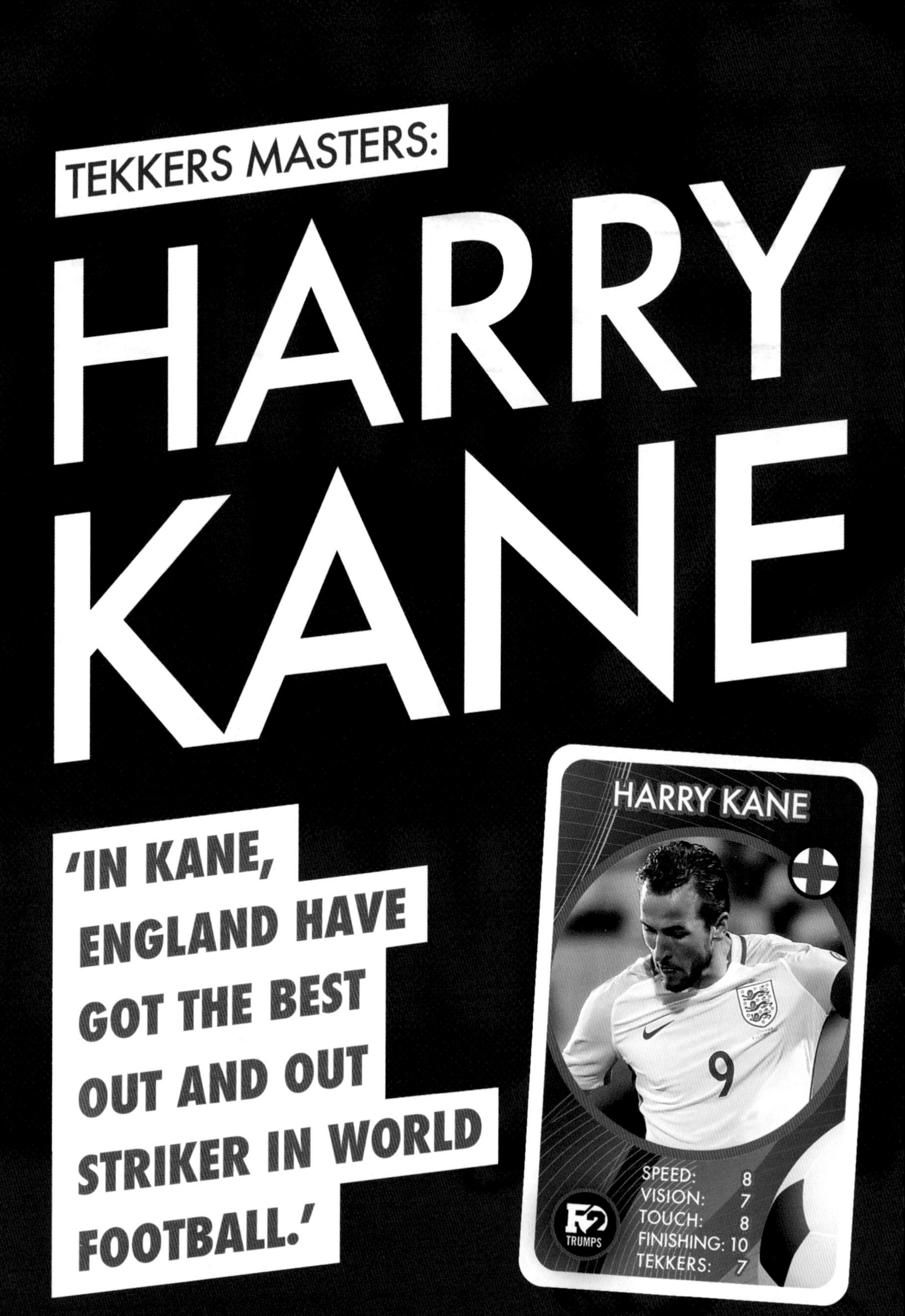
TEKKERS MASTERS:
HARRY
KANE
'IN KANE, ENGLAND HAVE GOT THE BEST OUT AND OUT STRIKER IN WORLD FOOTBALL.'
HARRY KANE
9
SPEED: 8
VISION: 7
TOUCH: 8
FINISHING: 10
TEKKERS: 7
F2
TRUMPS

Billy: You know, I remember that when we met the Spurs boss Mauricio Pochettino, he said 'I love the football – I don't understand footballers who don't love the football.' How this relates to Harry Kane is that I reckon he probably loves football more than anyone. It sure looks like he does! All he wants to do is score goals and he's so sure of himself. Every time he gets the ball, you know that it is in his head he believes he can score.

I reckon that if you're a striker with confidence, you will get 70 per cent of your chances. Confidence has other major advantages, though. If you're a striker who has no doubt that you will find the back of the net, it will seem like the ball will almost gravitate towards you.

You will just keep being in the right place at the right time. And I think this reflects in the goals that Harry Kane is scoring and in the records he's breaking.

Jez: Yeah, man. He clearly loves football. You can see he really, really wants to be out there on the pitch. He's pumped. He's still got that young, enthusiastic mentality every time he steps onto the pitch. He loves it.

He's come a long way, too, you know. You actually hear that about quite a few top players – they weren't at their very, very best as kids, but coaches had faith in them and they

'THERE IS NO ONE WHO BELIEVES IN HIMSELF MORE.'

worked hard and made it. They ended up blossoming later on.

Kane is obviously one of them. I remember when we were putting together a team of the year and we ended up debating whether to put in Neymar or Harry Kane. A couple of years ago, who would have thought, who would we be putting in: a Spurs player or Neymar!

But it's well deserved. I honestly think that in Kane England have got the best out-and-out striker in world football.

Billy: As a Spurs fan I've never seen anyone who can do what he can do in terms of striking the ball. What a player. His hunger is amazing. I would say to every young striker in the world, look at Harry Kane. If you can be even half as good as him you will be a great, great player.

He reminds me of various strikers we've had at Spurs down the years: Jürgen Klinnsman, Les Ferdinand and Teddy Sheringham. He's got a bit of what each of those three had. His movement is intelligent and amazing, his hold up play is incredible. His striking of the ball is obviously phenomenal.

It's true that he's not incredibly fast but he does so well with his body.

For instance, if he's racing with an opposing player, shoulder to shoulder, the first thing he'll do is get across them. So instantly it becomes a battle of strength and not speed. He's turned the battle into one he's more likely

You see it so many times, the ball goes over the top, it's a straight race for the defender with Harry Kane, but what he does is move into the defender's path. It becomes a battle for the ball. He thinks: 'I'll use my strength, even if you're faster than me, I'm going to get to the ball first.' Nine times out of 10 he gets to the ball faster.

I think is a really good message for kids. Although you can improve on your weaknesses, you can always play to your strengths as well. That's kind of what Harry Kane does.

Jez: Brilliant.

Billy: Harry Kane is a massive advocate for what we are saying in this book. There is no one who believes in himself more than Harry Kane. What he has got on other strikers is not just the ability but the belief as well.

'HIS STRIKING OF THE BALL IS OBVIOUSLY PHENOMENAL.'

THE JAMES VOLLEY

FACT FILE

ORIGIN: JAMES RODRÍGUEZ, 2014
SKILL TYPE: SHOT
DIFFICULTY RATING: 8
TEKKERS RATING: 10
FREQUENTLY USED BY: RODRÍGUEZ

Billy: Picture the scene: it's a boiling hot evening and you're playing under the lights in the first knockout stage of the World Cup finals in Brazil. The game is in the balance and the crowd are on their feet, you're standing at the edge of the box when your team-mate heads the ball towards you.

Instinctively you chest the ball to control it, pumping it on to your stronger foot; you then shift your weight and strike the ball as sweetly as you can, with all the swaz and technique you can muster. And then – bam – it's in the back of the net – a goal to savour and one of the most memorable goals ever to have been scored at a World Cup!

This, ladies and gentlemen, is the James Rodríguez volley...

GET YOUR CHEST RIGHT UNDER THE BALL

PLANT YOUR STANDING FOOT ALONGSIDE THE BALL

HIT THE BALL WITH POWER WITH THE OUTSIDE OF YOUR BOOT

FOLLOW THROUGH

WATCH IT SAIL OVER THE KEEPER AND INTO THE NET

BODY BEHIND THE BALL
PUMP THE BALL OUT IN FRONT OF YOU AND TOWARDS STRONGER FOOT
TIME YOUR SHOT TO HIT THE BALL AS IT FALLS
FOLLOW THROUGH WITH YOUR STRIKING FOOT

BILLY V JEZZA

MOST OUTRAGEOUS WORLD CUP MOMENTS

Billy: Jez I know your answer to this one and I'm going to agree with you. The most outrageous moment in World Cup history was... Jez, you tell them.

Jez: It's the Hand of God, when Diego Maradona blatantly punched the ball in against England in 1986. Who knows what could've happened that year if we'd won that tie.

Billy: The fact it happened in the same match as his wonder goal we mentioned earlier just makes it worse. It ruined England's hopes and what could otherwise have been a match that went down in football history for more positive reasons.

Jez: We had a great side that year - what a sickener.

Billy: I suppose another outrageous moment we could mention would be the Zidane headbutt at the 2006 World Cup final in Berlin. He absolutely floored Marco Materazzi. It was his last action in professional football – and what a way to go out.

Jez: You just couldn't write it. He had the perfect career and then he ended it with that. It was bizarre, And let's not forget when Roy Keane walked out of the 2002 World Cup. Another outrageous moment. Haha, he must have been proper angry to do that!

#TeamBilly: **Diego Maradona, 'Hand of God'**

#TeamJezza: **Diego Maradona, 'Hand of God'**

You: ____________________

F2 CHAPTER EIGHT

F2: WORLD CLASS

TACTICAL AWARENESS

Jez: Being aware of tactics is so important for football. Any of us can reel off the names of different positions or different formations, but unless you really, really understand what they mean in the heat of the battle, you're not getting the most out of your knowledge.

Again, watching football is the key to this. If you're at school or college level, it is good to watch the top players but also try and watch some stuff from lower leagues and even non-league, because the standard and style there will be closer to the level you'll be playing at. So watch the very best and also watch the lower leagues where it's more physical and less technical. Try and educate yourself on both.

Some people say you shouldn't think about football so much – just play it. I know what they mean, but I just think you should try to gain every advantage you can. If most of your opposition are not analysing the game as much as you are, right there you have an advantage over them. Having even a small intellectual advantage can make a difference.

Billy: Another important way to get aware of tactics is to train or play in a number of different positions. If you haven't trained and played in a number of positions, you will find it more or less impossible to relate to what your direct opponent might be thinking and doing.

So, say you're a winger, imagine the advantage you'll have if you've trained as a full-back! You'll know what's going on in his mind. So if you can understand your opponent you're one step closer to being able to outdo him. The only way to do that is to understand his position – and the only way to do that is by playing as him sometimes.

Get yourself coached in different positions. Otherwise it's just a mystery to you. If you want to be a better player, understand the players you're playing against. And if you want to understand tactics on match day, get your head around what these different terms mean.

The counter-attack

Jez: Man, you need plenty of confidence for this one! The reason is that the first stage is to draw the opposition into your defensive third. The idea is that they commit more players forward, leaving gaps. You then nick the ball from them and pile forward. Get the ball to your front players as quick as possible. Wingers in particular need to be ready to exploit the space.

The high press

Billy: This is as much about what you do without the ball as with it. Your team should play a really high defensive line and all the outfield guys need to be ready to harass and hustle their opponents, wherever the ball is. Your defence starts with your attackers. Think of Barcelona or Real Madrid at their best. The idea is that the closer to goal you win the ball, the less distance you need to cover to goal. But you need real fitness and stamina for this one – it's knackering!

Tiki-taka

Jez: This started in Spain but has spread. Arsenal were decent at it for a while. Here, we see short and swift intricate passing between players. To make it work, you need fluid movement and a midfield bustling with super-skilful players. But make sure at least one of the midfielders is a holder or you'll get destroyed. The strikers should be dragging opponents out of position.

The long ball

Billy: This is a basic one: from the deep positions you punt the ball forward towards a striker. Strikers need to be good in the air and physically strong. So this isn't a tactic that is particularly fashionable. But even the top clubs do it. Look at Sergio Aguero's opener in the Carabao Cup final.

Park the bus

Jez: This is another tactic some people sneer at, but top bosses like José Mourinho have used – and he's won a few trophies, hasn't he? Everyone know this means to play super-defensively. But how do you actually do it? Put a lot of players behind the ball, get defenders tucked into the centre and turn your wingers into full-backs. Normally, just one striker will be left up front. He will be isolated and will need to make the most of any chances that come his way.

TEKKERS MASTERS:

MARCUS RASHFORD

'WHEN HE'S ON THE BALL, HE'S EXCITING.'

Jez: I read that when Manchester United coaches used to collect this guy for training when he was a kid, when they arrived at his family's home they'd find him kicking a ball on to a garage roof and trying to control it as it came down. That's a perfect approach – even before training started he was already out there, refining his game.

What a great example of putting in the hours to take your game to the next level. Wayne Rooney used to do the same. After he burst onto the scene with that winning goal against Arsenal as a 16-year-old, he went home and spent the evening having a kickabout on the street with his mates.

He didn't even have to think about it; even when he was the talk of the top flight, he just wanted to get practising again. Rashford is the same.

Billy: We forget how young he is and how much growing and development there is to go. Because he's such a good player already, people look and think – oh, that's Marcus Rashford. That's how good he is going to be.

Jez: Yeah, it feels like he's been around for a while. Since he was at youth level at Man Utd they've been playing him levels ahead. Years above what he is, because they saw that he was too good for his own age group.

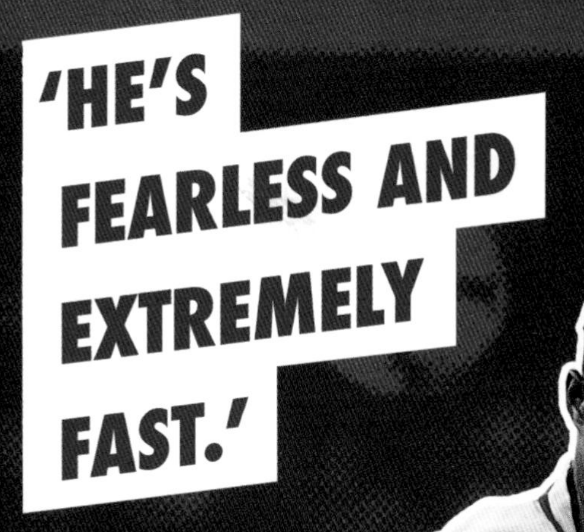
'HE'S
FEARLESS AND
EXTREMELY
FAST.'

Billy: It's already incredible how good he is but there's actually so much more to come. He's the type of player, you can tell that in two seasons' time when he's got that little bit of experience and he's that bit older, he's going to be a proper, proper force.

I mean, when he's on the ball, he's exciting. He's got so much pace. It's only a matter of time before he becomes one of the top players in the PL.

Jez: He plays at his best when he's got freedom. Definitely. That's when he's at his best. He's exciting, he's young and fresh. He's fearless and extremely fast.

We should be able to challenge for the World Cup with the players we have individually. I really believe that.

Billy: He is just a guy who really loves playing football. He works so hard and, like Beckham did, he stays behind after training every day. The basic truth is this: if you want to make it to the top, you have to work for it.

Jez: Even at such a tender age he's had to come through some adversity. At times last season people were being critical of him. He'd set such a high bar for himself that when he inevitably had some games where things didn't go quite so well for him, the haters began to hate.

Billy: But when you have an inherent base of self-confidence, you can get through these sorts of patches.

Jez: Self-assurance is gold, though, it really is. That's one thing you can be sure of: any player in the world is much better confident than lacking confidence. That applies to anyone. So if you're confident in yourself, you will always be better than if you're not confident in yourself.

So just try to be the best you can be. Measure yourself against yourself. I don't know how many clubs employ full-time psychologists but if clubs aren't implementing that then they're missing a trick.

If I was running a football club, or if I was a manager, the first thing I'd want to do was employ someone who can get the players' minds in order. To get them confident, just like Rashford is.

Billy: And he can take plenty of confidence from the fact that Ronaldo, the Brazilian legend, has said he sees a lot of himself in Rashford. That's praise indeed – a Tekkers Master of the past bigging up a Tekkers Master of the present and future.

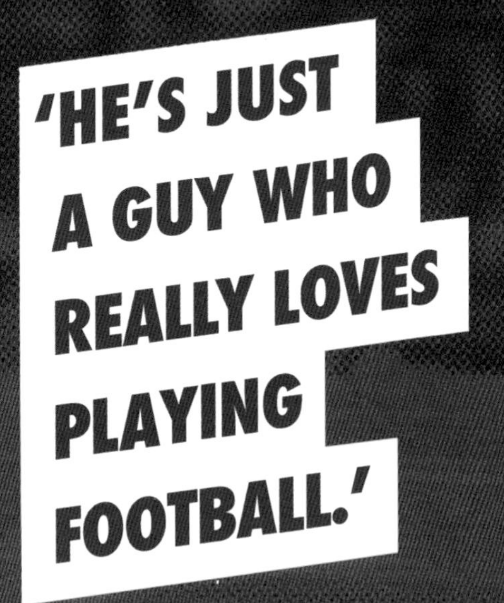

GET THE SKILLS:

THE PANENKA

FACT FILE

ORIGIN: ANTONÍN PANENKA, YUGOSLAVIA, 1976
SKILL TYPE: SHOT
DIFFICULTY RATING: 6
TEKKERS RATING: 8
FREQUENTLY USED BY: PIRLO, SANCHEZ, ZIDANE, MESSI

Jez: There are two sides to the Panenka penalty – one's all about technique whilst the other is about mentality. Pirlo, Zidane, Alexis Sànchez – only the biggest players can get away with such an audacious piece of skill and if you don't hold your nerve then it can go horribly wrong. I mean, who can forget Pirlo's penalty against England at the 2012 Euros? It was coolness personified.

Deception and elevation are the key ingredients for the perfect Panenka. Place the ball down, pick your spot, run up to the ball and then: dink. But it's not just any old dink; it needs to have enough power and elevation to float into the net and enough height to miss the keeper's flailng feet as he dives to one of the corners. From Antonín Panenka to Lionel Messi, here's how it's done.

F2

RUN UP TO THE BALL AT A
SLIGHT ANGLE
CHECK YOUR SHOT AND LIGHTLY
CHIP THE BALL AT ITS BASE
FOLLOW THROUGH

SWING YOUR LEG BACK AS IF
TO STRIKE IT POWERFULLY

PLANT YOUR STRIKING FOOT ON THE
GROUND TO ENSURE ELEVATION

KEEP CALM AND RUN UP TO THE BALL

CHECK YOUR SHOOTING FOOT AND PLACE IT AT THE BASE OF THE BALL

FOLLOW THROUGH AND WATCH THE BALL SAIL OVER THE KEEPER

DECEPTION FIRST...

...AND THEN ELEVATION

CELEBRATE AS COOLY AS
YOU LIKE

BILLY V JEZZA

LEGENDS

Billy: There's so many true legends of the game that have graced the World Cup, the best players ever: Cruyff, Zidane, Eusebio, Pelé, Maradona, Beckham, both Ronaldos, Maldini, Beckenbauer, Koeman, Messi, the list is endless...

Jez: But what about those legends who didn't play in the World Cup?

Billy: Great question Jez, a personal favourite, David Ginola!

Jez: Ryan Giggs!

Billy: George Best!

Jez: George Weah!

Billy: Jez....Eric Cantona!

Jez: Cantona never played in the World Cup? That's criminal!

#TeamBilly: David Ginola

#TeamJezza: Ryan Giggs

You: ______________________

J-E
adidas

CHAPTER NINE

CREATING YOUR BRAND

Billy: Jez, if I asked you to name me a footballer whose name is synonymous with crazy hairstyles, who would you say?

Jez: Hmm... I'd go with Paul Pogba. Am I right?

Billy: Correct – and the fact you got that answer right first time shows how strong Pogba's brand is. After all, there's no shortage of memorable hairstyles in football. But Pogba has become the most standout name in that regard. Why? Because he's got a strong brand.

Different players have different brands. Cristiano Ronaldo's is based on style. He looks the business on and off the pitch, and has his CR7 range

of clothes and toiletries. That's a brand right there.

Jez: Yes. Then there's Neymar. When he made his move to Paris Saint-Germain it was for a huge fee – £200 million. PSG were happy to pay that because they knew that as well as bringing them so much on the field, Neymar would offer a lot off the pitch, too. When he signed, PSG got 5.3 million more followers on social media. It all works for the man himself, too – he's got 20 global brand partners.

Billy: There are other players with brands, too. Think of a footballer who loves dogs and you're straightaway thinking of Alexis Sanchez. Atom and Humber have become stars in their own rights.

Jez: This is all part of the fun of the game. Making yourself stand out and developing an individual identity for yourself. Some players do with tattoos, or by dyeing their hair. There's many ways. Plus, there's building brands like Rascal and The F2...

Billy: Well, indeed. So what is a brand? I think the best way to define it is to look at our story: I was a solo freestyler, tied to Tottenham. Jez was a solo freestyler, who'd been on Britain's Got Talent. I was Billy

Wingrove, he was Jeremy Lynch. Would people watch a YouTube channel or buy a brand of clothes, called 'Billy Wingrove' or 'Jeremy Lynch'? They wouldn't.

We knew that we had something cool, but how could we turn it into a brand? We decided to call ourselves The F2. As soon as you get a name and create a logo, that is the brand. It becomes bigger than yourself.

Jez: How should people get started?

Billy: To get there, you need to know exactly what you're doing it for and what the outcome is you're after. Then you have to create yourself some proper brand guidelines: what are you prepared to do, how do you intend to grow?

Jez: Yeah, and the other important thing to do early is to look for a gap in the market. Where is there demand that isn't being met? Try and meet the demand. So for me and Bill, there had never been any kind of football double act before, and no one was doing entertaining football content either. That was the gap we identified.

Lots of people are doing it now because we created that footprint but we were the pioneers. We thought that people would be entertained by

what we wanted to do and therefore it would meet a demand.

So here's another golden rule: try to find the gap and try to meet the demand.

Billy: You've got to think of a name and a logo that fits perfectly with your plan. You've got to think of colours and design that fit with what you're offering. If you're going to be outrageous, use outrageous colours and designs. If you're aiming for a younger audience, devise a name and design that appeals to them.

Get to know 100 per cent what your brand is about and identify exactly what you're offering. How are you going to be different? Because there's no two ways about it: to stand out you need to be unique.

Jez: Here's something else to never, ever lose sight of: the most important thing is your product. Ultimately, most people who watch our videos are watching because they're a good product. Most people who buy Rascal are buying it because it's a good product.

Even if they're our most dedicated fans, they're not really watching for us, they're watching for their own entertainment. So the service has to be good. You can do all the collaborations, marketing and promotion in the world, you can get millions of eyes on your product, but if it's not good, it's not going to succeed.

Billy: So remember: Make sure your product is good.

Jez: Once you've got the good product, you want to look at marketing it. Market it well. Be smart. Understand your consumers, their minds and what they want. And then give it to them.

Billy: So say you've got going, and you've had a bit of success. You want to know where you're going to go next. Get methodical, guys. Create a five-year strategy. Always ask yourself where you want it to be in five years.

I remember our first target was to get to 80,000 subscribers, because we'd seen another channel with that many. It seemed a huge amount of subscribers at the time, it just all seemed so far away.

To get there, we had to work out who we were and what we'd offer. Most other football YouTubers at the time were doing one thing, so we decided to go for more of an all-rounder. We knew we could play football, and do tricks, and perform tekkers and have the outrageous banter.

No one out there was ticking all of those boxes. So we created a mixed product. Fans come and watch us for different reasons, some of them come for the banter, some to watch tutorials, some just to watch our mad tekkers. We were offering it all.

Jez: So that was what our early goals were about. But we kept setting new goals all the time.

Billy: We did. Pretty soon, we noticed that KSI had 6m subscribers and drove a Lamborghini. He had a really high profile. We looked at all that and decided to set him as our benchmark.

That was our second goal. When we passed our first milestone of 80,000 subscribers, we set a new target: to get to 6m subscribers, just like KSI. Now we're sitting on 7m subscribers. It's insane!

Jez: And now we want nothing less than to be the number one football channel for ever.

Billy: You know, the rules we will be following to make that happen are the same ones you should be following even in the early days.

One of them is to keep asking yourself questions. Can I do better? What am I doing wrong? What is working for me that I can improve on? How can I adapt as the market changes? Keep asking yourself these questions every day. I know we will be.

Jez: If something doesn't work, it doesn't mean it hasn't been a success. Success can mean learning. If you make a mistake you learn from that mistake. So look at any mistake in a positive way, like we have.

Billy: Probably the trailblazer for footballing branding during my

lifetime is David Beckham, who was a star on and off the pitch. We, too, have worked hard on our brand. The success we've enjoyed has come in part because we knew what our identity was, what we were about, and then stuck with it.

Jez: But listen, never get confused about what comes first. The brand or the work? Of course, it's the work. These players we are talking about, like Pogba, are at the top of their game. They've worked on their game day in, day out, for year after year.

Billy: You took the words right out of my mouth, Jez. The game comes first, then the brand. Never get your priorities mixed up. That's like expecting to lift the World Cup because you've got your brand sorted. It's not how life works.

Jez: Final word on this: on a football team basis, I think carrying yourself as a leader or motivator is one brand you'd be really right to aim for. There's not a football team in the world that doesn't need leadership and motivation. Find out more in the next chapter.

TEKKERS MASTERS:

ROBERT LEWANDOWSKI

'IN THE BOX HE'S DEADLY. HE SCORES SO MANY GOALS.'

Billy: He scores goals, doesn't he?

Jez: Does he really, Bill? I never knew that!

Billy: But it's true! This guy scores goals. That's basically him. He has scored goals all of his life. He's quite simply a complete striker.

And you know the really special thing about him? The really good thing is that he can do it on the big stage. That's important. To be the very best, you've got to prove your worth in the top, top games. He's one of those guys.

I read an insane statistic the other day. It was that Theo Walcott played in two cup finals for Arsenal, and scored in both, while between them, Thierry Henry and Dennis Bergkamp played in 10 cup finals for Arsenal, and neither scored in any of them.

Surprising, eh? Now don't get me wrong: Bergkamp and Henry are truly incredible players and you have to look at the wider context here. Walcott, great as he is, might not have been marked as tightly in those finals as Henry and Bergkamp would have been in theirs.

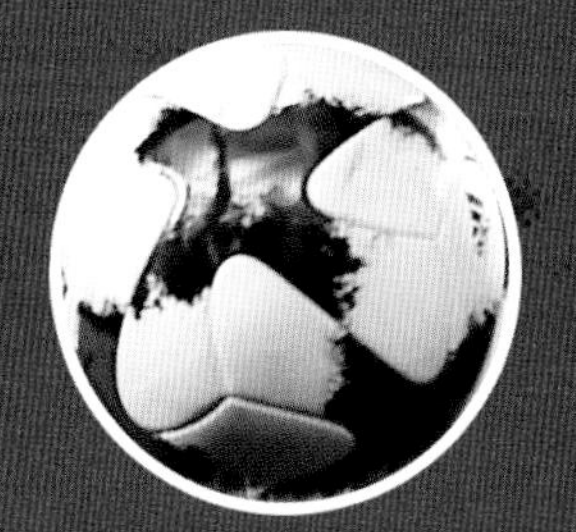

But it still shows you that big games can really be a test for any player: in the run-up you get all the nerves, all the anxiety. Often, three days before the game you can't sleep. You're excited, you're anxious, you're being confronted by how much you want it.

All of that build up is channelled into the game. There's so much pressure. Some players are not fazed by the pressure, some players are fazed. But then there's a third category, who positively embrace the pressure. They think: this is my time to shine. But some players just can and do perform in those big games. Lewandowski is one of them.

Jez: Yeah, he's got it all, everything you need to be a number nine. Everything you need physically and psychologically. He's tall, he's incredible in the air. He keeps himself in perfect shape. He's intelligent and he keeps his confidence up all the time.

No wonder he's been consistently one of the best in the world. He's not a flash in the pan, he's the real deal who has stood the test of time. Look, there have been plenty of players who have managed to have one amazing season and then they never live up to it. For him to keep doing it at the highest level, including the Champions League, is unreal.

Billy: He's dangerous all over the attack. He can introduce team-mates and hold up the ball. In the box he's deadly. He scores so many goals. He's tall and he's big. So when he comes up against big centre-backs he can hold his own. He's just a complete striker.

Jez: He works really hard on and off the pitch. He doesn't leave anything to chance, or hope for a bit of luck. Even though luck can happen.

Billy: How important is luck, would you say?

Jez: Mate, I think in this game you need a combination of a lot of hard work and a bit of luck. So hard work does pay off in the long run.

> **'HE SCORED FIVE GOALS IN UNDER NINE MINUTES. HOW CAN YOU EVEN DO THAT?'**

But then there are variables that you cannot necessarily control. Maybe something like your family being sufficiently supportive for you to be able to make it. Or not. Things like that you cannot really control. You can't control luck, either. It comes and it goes, you know?

So focus on what you can control. Like Lewandowski has his whole career.

Billy: For me, his finest hour must be when he came on as a substitute at half-time for Bayern Munich, when they were losing 1-0 to Wolfsburg. He scored five goals in under nine minutes. How can you even do that? You don't just do something like that, do you? But he did.

Jez: He did. Because he's Lewandowski!

GET THE SKILLS:

THE LYNCH LEVIOSA

FACT FILE

ORIGIN: JEREMY LYNCH
SKILL TYPE: DRIBBLE
DIFFICULTY RATING: 9
TEKKERS RATING: 10
FREQUENTLY USED BY:
JEREMY LYNCH

Jez: This skill gives a new meaning to the term 'twisted blood'. In fact it not only twists the defender's blood, but positively ties their blood in knots! Although the Leviosa might look difficult, with a bit of practice it's easy to nail. It's all about poise and speed, and being sharp on the turn. Just make sure you don't tie yourself up in knots trying to perform it on the pitch!

Perfect for getting out of a tricky spot on the wing or when you need to lift your game on the touchline, here's how it's done...

WITH THE OUTSIDE OF YOUR STRONGER FOOT, DRAG THE BALL ACROSS YOUR BODY

BRING YOUR OTHER FOOT ACROSS THE BALL, STEPPING OVER IT

DRAG THE BALL BACK WITH YOUR STRONGER FOOT, OPENING UP YOUR BODY AS YOU DO SO

QUICKLY FLICK THE BALL BEHIND YOU WITH THE BACK OF YOUR HEEL

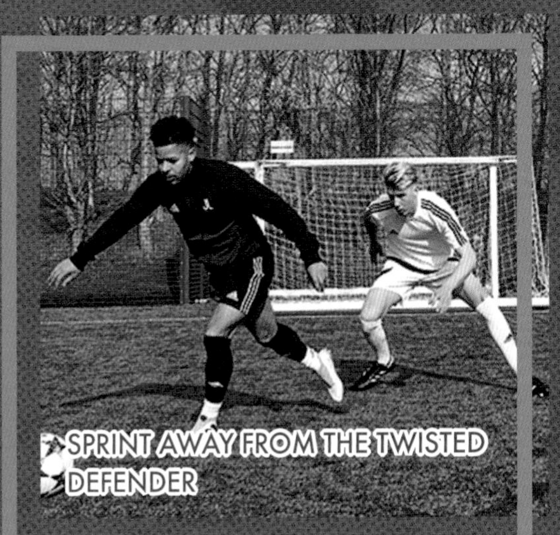

SPRINT AWAY FROM THE TWISTED DEFENDER

DRAG THE BALL ACROSS YOUR BODY
STEP OVER THE BALL
DRAG THE BALL BACK
TURN AND FLICK THE BALL BEHIND YOU

DRAG...
DRAG BACK...
BALL BACK BEHIND YOU
STEP OVER...
OPEN YOUR BODY
AND SPRINT AWAY

BILLY V JEZZA

BEST WORLD CUP MATCH

Billy: So I'll go with England v Argentina in 1998. What a game, Jez. WHAT a game. It had everything: goals... great goals... disallowed goals... penalties... sendings off, the works.

From the high of Michael Owen's famous goal when he ran nearly the length of the field, to the low of England going out on penalties yet again, via the controversy of David Beckham being sent off for kicking Diego Simeone.

Jez: Yeah, that match had more incident in it than you sometimes get in a whole tournament. But that entire World Cup was just mind-blowing.

I'm going to go with the final between Brazil and France that year. There was so much drama even before kick off, with Ronaldo being unwell. The game was meant to be all about Ronaldo v Zidane – that face off. As it turned out, Zidane put on a masterclass. That's a stand out World Cup game for me.

#TeamBilly: England v Argentina, 1998

#TeamJezza: France v Brazil, 1998

You: ____________________

adidas

CHAPTER TEN

F2: WORLD CLASS

MOTIVATION AND PSYCHOLOGY

Billy: Motivation is so important. You can see when two teams are out on the pitch which of them is most up for it. Think of when Leicester City won the league. That was an unbelievable story. When that season kicked off, no one was talking about them even finishing in the top half, let alone walking off with the league title!

But that's exactly what they did. There's a lot of reasons why. I'd say a big one was that they were so motivated. Every game they seemed absolutely pumped to be out there. I see the same with Spurs under Pochettino, too. Unreal levels of motivation.

Jez: And it's all in the mind, Bill. So much of what happens on the pitch is actually going on right inside the heads of the players. You can turn this to your advantage before the game even kicks off. Think about how you are going to come across to the opposition. If you look scared, they will see that and it will make them feel bolder. But if you carry yourself with confidence, your opponents will pick up on that.

Billy: There's a deeper lesson to this, too. I've seen experts say that you can go a long way to determining your mood by your body language and facial expression. If you stand tall, with your shoulders wide, that positive body language will start to flush your body with real confidence. The same goes for facial expression, even if you are feeling a bit nervous, just put on the best 'game face' that you can muster. It will make a really positive difference.

Jez: So get an upright posture with a confident gait. A gait means the way you walk. Also, hold your head up. It should be a bit above horizontal, ideally. Put this book down now and try this walk and posture a few times. Then try walking with your shoulder

slouched and your head down. See how each posture makes you feel – you'll notice the difference.

Billy: Do the bold stance on match day. Stand as dominantly as you can before kick-off. You can see how the pros do this in the tunnel before a game and then out on the field as they line up. Follow their example. Like Jez said, get your head up, your shoulders strong and puff your chest out. Some football managers say that the game is 75 per cent about confidence. That's huge!

A lot of the psychology comes into play between games, too – and between training sessions. Because it simply doesn't matter how much you love playing football, there will be days when your head tells you to give it a miss and just relax on the sofa. It will tempt you into giving training or practice a miss and spending the day watching TV or playing Fifa.

Jez: That's right, Bill. It's the same for everyone: whether it's a kid kicking the ball around his local park or us two, or the world's biggest names, everyone has days where they struggle to get motivated.

Just remind yourself why you are doing it. Remember that you will only really get out of football what you put into it. It's an honest, democratic game: it generally gives you back what you have put into it.

There are many different ways of motivating yourself. Watch videos of your favourite players doing what they do. Listen to music to pump yourself up. Set yourself a new goal for the day. Different things work for different players – find the one that works for you.

Billy: Another aspect of the psychology is dealing with the haters that you can attract as you make a success of yourself. I look at it this way – the better you get, the more haters you will attract. This is sad but true. With success and recognition you get a lot of really nice things. We feel so blessed and fortunate to have had such a great ride since we formed the F2.

But as more and more people get to know you, negative people will come out of the woodwork and throw unpleasant things at you. You can't have one without the other. We really wish you could, but the simple truth is that you can't.

Jez: To be honest, it's only ever one or two negative comments compared to hundreds and thousands of positive ones. I always think you can turn a negative into a positive anyway. Sometimes it can drive you on even more.

Billy: You just have to learn how to tune out this sort of negativity. A good way to do this is to remind yourself that if someone says something horrible to you, it's not actually you they are talking about – it's themselves.

Jez: Yeah. They're just projecting on to you the negativity floating around in their own mind. So just remind yourself that whatever they say about you, it's not about you, it's about them. Whatever you do, don't let them drag you down to their level. Then they've won.

Billy: Look at players like Messi and Ronaldo, particularly Ronaldo. Do you think he's always had a positive reaction? But he's become a master at taking negative energy and turning it into a positive. He's not let a minority bully him or take away his dreams. I think this is something we can all learn from.

Jez: Absolutely, if you're suffering from someone else's negativity, then remember you're not alone, things will get better with time, so hold your head high, be yourself and be more Ronaldo! It's one of the many attributes that have turned this man into the incredible, world-class footballer he is. And if it's good enough for him, then it might just work for the rest of us.

Billy: Nice, Jez! Now there's a positive message to end on. Be more Ronaldo!

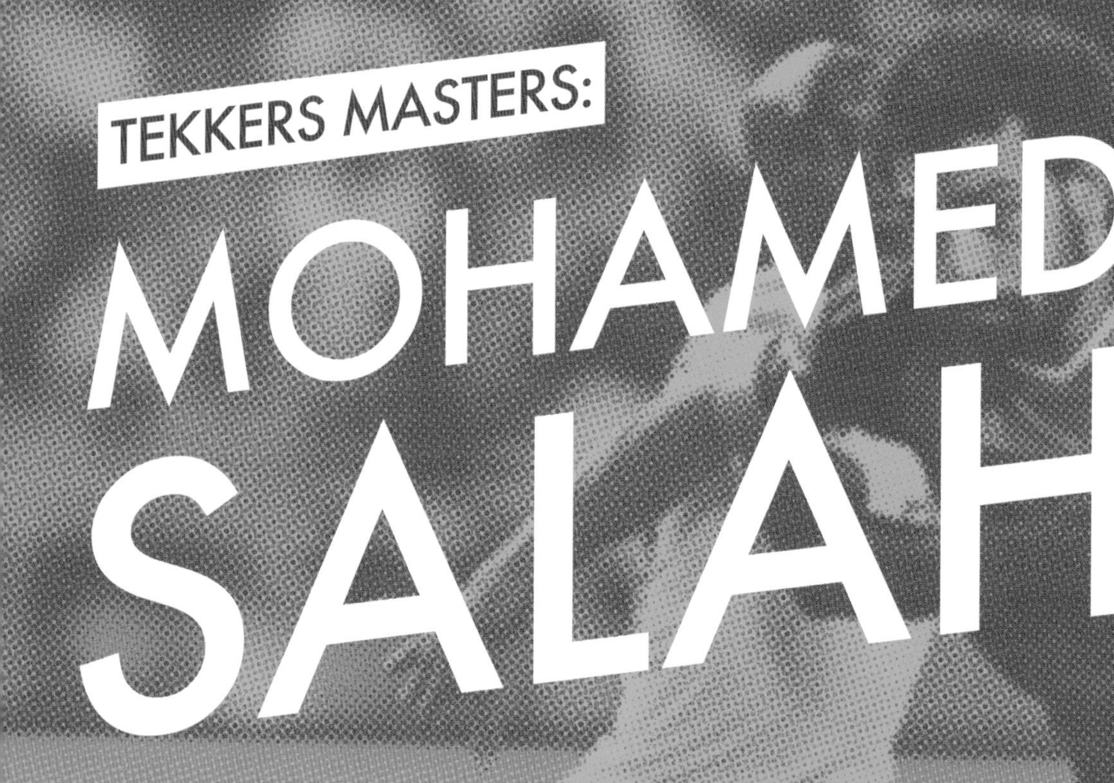

TEKKERS MASTERS: MOHAMED SALAH

'IF LIVERPOOL ARE ON I'LL WATCH THEM JUST TO SEE MO SALAH.'

Billy: You know, I watch him play and this is going to sound absurd, but I can see Messi-type features in him. The way he dribbles with the ball, the way he is so direct. His change of pace. That left-foot finishing. I can see similarities.

Jez: Hmmm, I don't so much get the comparison.

Billy: Oh, I'm not comparing him. We know Messi is probably the best player of all time. We know that Mo Salah is one of those players who can win you a game. He can create something out of nothing.

Jez: He's really good and he's having a blinding season. But I'm still waiting to see what will happen. For me, the jury is still out. I think he's the real deal. Time will tell. I'm not going to be throwing too much praise all over this guy until I've seen more.

Billy: Fair enough, mate. But I'm ready to unleash the praise right now! I'm not a Liverpool fan but if Liverpool are on I'll watch them just to see Mo Salah. That's the best compliment you can pay a player, really.

I'd say the same about Coutinho when he was there. I'd be looking forward to seeing those two. As I say, there have been quite a few of these at Anfield down the years. Steven Gerrard would be in that category.

You'd switch on just to see what he could do. Fernando Torres was another one, and so was Luis Suárez.

They could create something out of nothing, just when it was needed. Players like these are the real 'box office' stars, the ones who will draw in a big audience for a game. Television companies love them, fans love them and so do their team-mates and coaches.

Jez: Another thing about Salah is that he can deliver when the pressure is on. Look at what he did against Spurs last season. That stoppage time goal took real balls – and it was him who had opened the scoring at the start of the game.

For the second strike, he was quality. He collected the ball on the right side of the box, and then jinked his way past four defenders. They didn't know what he was going to do next.

In fact, the key to the goal was unpredictability. Just like the top attackers in the world do, he kept everyone guessing as to what he was going to do next. Then he slid through and lifted the ball over Hugo Lloris from the tightest of angles.

'HE CAN DELIVER WHEN THE PRESSURE IS ON.'

Billy: That's entertainment right there! He's also done it on the international stage for Egypt. It was his two goals against Congo that took Egypt to their first World Cup finals tournament since 1990. Making history.

The stats are really promising for him, too. He is the fastest Liverpool player to hit the 20-goal mark in the Premier League. It took him 25 games to do it – that's two games quicker than Fernando Torres and Daniel Sturridge. The numbers don't lie.

He's got a reputation as being very modest – and this is something I'd like to add to the list of qualities that help make you world class. It's easy to look at the top players and see them as superstars, full of self-confidence. And yeah, they are confident, you have to be to make it to the top.

But they will also have a slice of modesty in them, if you see what I mean. It's that humility that makes you want to work hard, to listen to advice, to always be trying to improve.

Jez: I'd agree with that, actually. These are very wise words. Combine confidence with modesty. Create a healthy balance of those two qualities and you can really take your game to that next level.

Okay, so maybe this guy can go on to be the best in Britain. Maybe. It will be exciting to watch. Is there anything better than seeing a player as he develops and flourishes in the game? He's one to watch this guy, I'll say that.

GET THE SKILLS:

RONALDO CHOP

FACT FILE

ORIGIN: CRISTIANO RONALDO
SKILL TYPE: DRIBBLE
DIFFICULTY RATING: 7
TEKKERS RATING: 9
FREQUENTLY USED BY:
CRISTIANO RONALDO

Jez: Cristiano Ronaldo has more moves than a chess grand master, but this one is probably his signature skill. The Ronaldo Chop is beautiful in its simplicity and you can use it in a game situation to change the direction of an attack in the wink of an eye. (See what I did there?!)

There are two important tips to bear in mind. First, you need to anticipate the defender coming across in front of you for maximum effect. Second, you need to hit the ball with enough force to get it a few feet away from you so that you're free to sprint on to it. That's the basics, now get out there and practise. Chop, chop!

RUN AT PACE
HIT THE BALL WITH YOUR INSTEP
BEHIND YOUR OTHER LEG...
... TO ACCELERATE ON TO IT

JUMP BOTH FEET IN THE AIR

...WITH ENOUGH POWER TO
GIVE YOU ROOM...

RUN AT PACE

AS THE DEFENDER MOVES TO INTERCEPT...

JUMP AND AS YOU LAND...

KNOCK THE BALL WITH YOUR INSTEP BEHIND YOUR OTHER LEG

HIT THE BALL FAR ENOUGH AWAY...
THAT YOU CAN RUN ON TO IT
AFTERBURNERS!

OUTRO

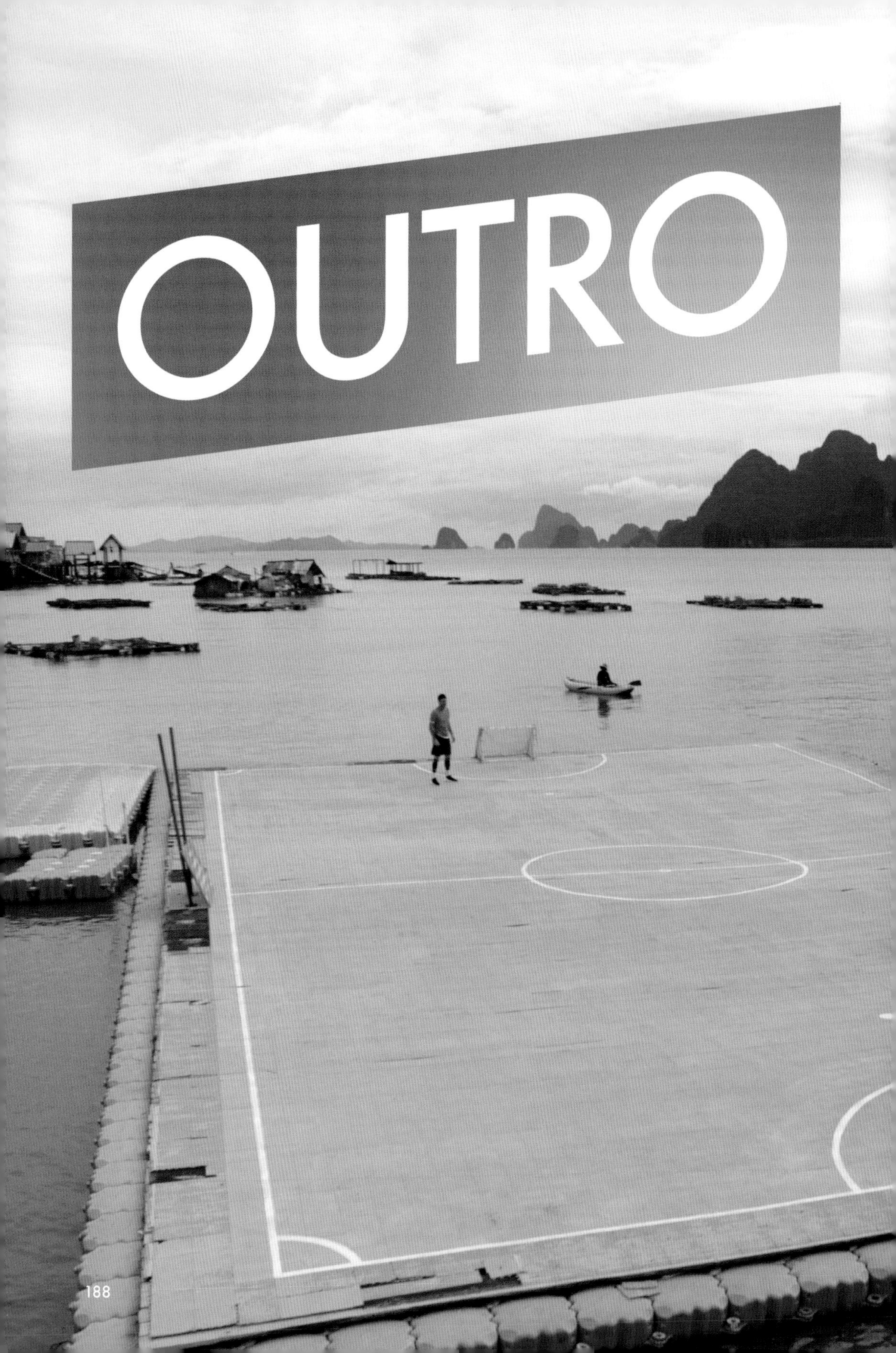

Guys, the referee is checking his watch and he's about to blow his whistle.

But before we call time on this book, we wanted to check in with you and amplify one of the main messages of these pages.

Everyone who wants to play football wants to be world class. What sort of person would set out to be average at what they do? It doesn't even make sense!

So yes, we hope the tips in this book will help propel you to the very top of the game. If you work hard, take good advice, and practice like your life depends on it, you could be the next Lionel Messi or Cristiano Ronaldo.

But as we've said, there is whole other way of defining 'world class'. This involves becoming not necessarily the best in the world, but the best you can be. It means looking at your very highest potential and doing everything you can to reach it.

So keep working and practising. Stay humble and stay true to yourself. Professional contracts and trophies are brilliant – but being all you can be is just as golden.

Love, peace and tekkers, The F2.

adidas
ADV / 91-17
RESPECT
adidas
JL
BW
adidas
BW
RASCAL

ACKNOWLEDGEMENTS

Our families have supported and loved us from the get go. We owe them a huge debt of gratitude. Life has given both of us so many brilliant moments but it has also thrown us challenges. You guys have been there for us through good times and bad. You really are elite level – thank you so much.

We'd like to say a big thank you to the team at Blink Publishing: our editor Matt Phillips; designer Steve Leard; photographers Dan Rouse and Chris Macchi, Ben Dunn, Perminder Mann, Joel Simons, Dominic Aveiro, Alba Proko, Emily Rough, Andrew Sauerwine, Lizzie Dorney- Kingdom, Lisa Hoare, Justine Taylor and Ian Prior. Thanks to [illegible]as Newkey-Burden for once more helping us bring our story to life.

Big thanks to the team at F2 HQ: Sam Bayford, Ben Goldhagen, the incredible team at adidas, all the brands, agencies and teams we work with. Every day you support what we do and make our journey more exciting. Thanks also to all the players, managers and other stars who have been part of our videos. It blows our minds to have worked with you!

Finally, thank you to you – the person reading this. The F2 Family is the greatest fan-base on the planet – a truly world-class community. Without you we could not have done any of this. Thanks for your support and so many brilliant memories. We wish you every success and happiness.

PHOTOGRAPHY CREDITS

All images courtesy of The F2, except the following:

Dan Rouse: 6–7, 22–23, 28, 36–37, 38–39, 46, 54–55, 56–57, 72–73, 74–75, 90–91, 92–93, 96, 118–119, 120–121, 134–135, 136–137, 138,139, 150–151, 152–153, 155, 161, 168–169, 170–171, 172, 173, 184–185, 186–187, 190–191

Chris Macchi: 8–9,10,11, 12–13, 24, 25, 26–27, 31, 44–45, 58, 59, 60–61, 64, 67, 77, 78, 80–81, 94, 97, 98, 99, 108–109, 111, 122, 123, 124–125, 127, 128, 129, 140–141, 143, 154, 156–157, 158, 160, 175–175, 177, 178, 179, 188–189, 190–191

Getty Images: 15, 17, 18, 19, 20, 24, 25, 29, 30, 32, 33, 35, 41, 47, 50–51, 53, 58, 59, 63, 66, 68–69, 70, 76, 78–79, 83, 84, 86–87, 89, 95, 96, 97, 99, 100, 106, 112, 113, 114–115, 116, 123, 130–131, 132, 138, 144, 145, 146–147, 148, 154, 155, 159, 163, 164–165, 166, 173, 180–181, 182, 190–191

HALF-TIME ACTIVITIES ANSWERS

Spot the ball: H2

Spot the difference:

Word search:

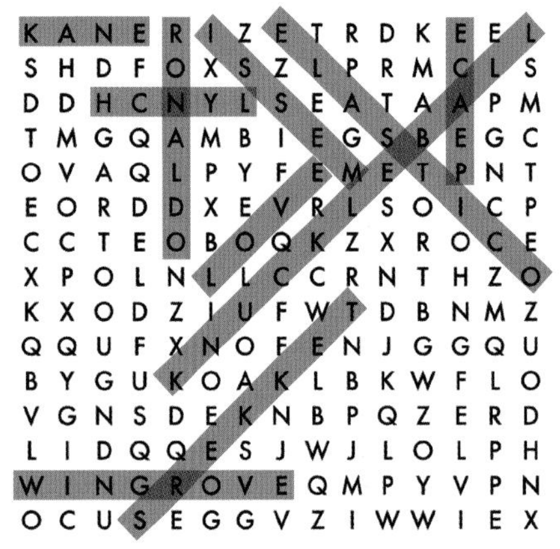

F2 quiz:

1. Bill
2. In The Hands of the Gods
3. Bill
4. Britain's Got Talent
5. False
6. The F2 Go To Hollywood
7. Lewis Hamilton
8. Ankle
9. Wingrove
10. Lynch
11. F2: World of Football: How to Play Like a Pro
12. Spurs
13. Michael Jackson
14. Rascal
15. Jez
16. Mark Upson
17. 2010
18. UK Entertainment Act of the Year
19. Barcelona
20. The FIFA Ballon d'Or

Crossword:

Across
1. Spain
4. False
7. Swaz
9. Gabonese
10. Stamina
11. Tekkers
13. Brazil
14. YouTube
15. Ozil
16. Etihad

Down
2. Alexis
3. Kane
4. Fifa
5. Hazard
6. Practise
8. Wembley
12. Rabona
13. Bins

World Cup quiz:

1. 4
2. 32
3. Top scorer
4. World War II
5. Pelé
6. 1966
7. True
8. 1930
9. Japan
10. Fifa World Cup Trophy
11. Three-banded armadillo
12. False
13. Brazil
14. James Rodríguez
15. South Africa
16. Thomas Müller
17. Steven Gerrard
18. Roy Hodgson
19. Mexico, Costa Rica, USA, Nigeria or China.
20. 18